THE CAMBRIDGE MISCELLANY

XIX

CHARLES LAMB

T0364340

CHARLES LAMB
AND HIS CONTEMPORARIES

BY

EDMUND BLUNDEN

CAMBRIDGE
AT THE UNIVERSITY PRESS
1937

CAMBRIDGE UNIVERSITY PRESS
Cambridge, New York, Melbourne, Madrid, Cape Town,
Singapore, São Paulo, Delhi, Tokyo, Mexico City

Cambridge University Press
The Edinburgh Building, Cambridge CB2 8RU, UK

Published in the United States of America by
Cambridge University Press, New York

www.cambridge.org
Information on this title: www.cambridge.org/9781107680104

First published 1937
First paperback edition 2011

A catalogue record for this publication is available from the British Library

ISBN 978-1-107-68010-4 Paperback

CONTENTS

PREFACE

It was in my mind to attempt a large account of Charles Lamb and to proceed with researches for that purpose, when the Master and Fellows of Trinity College honoured me with an invitation to give the Clark Lectures of 1932; and the subject of Lamb being uppermost, I perhaps injudiciously offered it. I say injudiciously because the occasion did not seem to require the kind of diurnal and detailed reconsideration which I had begun to see shaping itself to my hand; a series of lectures for an audience however learned and sympathetic would mean not a collection but a selection of topics and biographical circumstances. My hosts accepted my proposed subject, and the ensuing pages are the after-effect of their benevolence. I am delighted to record here my gratitude for the honour done to me by the Master and Fellows, as to a line of men of letters before me, and to add that, whatever the fate of the lectures may be, the lecturer's memory has been enriched by a series of personal experiences, kind beyond his deservings. May I thank, too, the members of the audience who supported me (in spite of a busy term, and my failure to master the acoustic mysteries of the Hall of Trinity) with such intrepid attention?

The scope, then, of this book is that of a sketch; the biographical element is mainly confined to the needs of a critical theme. I have not called up all the reserves of information for it, although I have usually endeavoured not to employ the most battered references and anecdotes. The text of the lectures is, with a few adjustments found necessary on revision, that which was spoken; but I have added footnotes. Were there more of these, they might provide some relief to the persistent questioning in the text; for, like Mr F. V. Morley, who was exploring the psychological history of "Lamb before Elia" while I was moving nearly in a parallel with him, I have been mainly aware of the peculiar hazard of all dogmatizing on the inwardness of Lamb the mystificator. Of course I have ventured some round decisions; but no lecturer was ever complete without them, and Lamb would have winked at them.

This world being handicapped with a 24-hour day, and this hand being already a trifle obstinate and erratic, it may be that the present volume will remain my only lengthy observation on Charles Lamb; were I to go farther, and accom-

plish an elaborate renovation, one aspect would
be unaltered. I mean the great honour and
admiration which all have for Mr E. V. Lucas as
Lamb's editor and biographer. His work is beyond praise; and it is only the fact that there are
in the course of time shiftings of idea, and various
possibilities of treatment, and—even after his
wonderfully vigilant enquiries—discoveries of
letters, documents, writings to be made, that
allows me to think of any experiment in Elian
biography by me or anybody, such short reviews
as the present excepted. I lament intensely the
loss of Mrs G. A. Anderson, who above all
people realized what Mr Lucas himself had not
recaptured of Lamb's friendships and interests,
and who studied to complete the portrait. "Thou
shouldst have longer lived!" or shall I say,
varying another of Lamb's utterances, "Mild
G. A. A.! thou hast now thy C. L. in heaven".

E. B.

1933

CHAPTER I

AN EIGHTEENTH-CENTURY CHILDHOOD

There is some reason to anticipate the general disappearance from this world of the romantic man, not in our time, no doubt, but some time before the dark and cold conclusion of the whole solecism. There may come an altered human type, which, liberated from the obscurities which actuate our emotions, and set in clear control of physical and economical conditions, will have no more concern with our kind of dreaming triumphs and picturesque imperfections than a thermometer. Already one may observe some hints of a metamorphosis. To many of my generation, the fact of war is a considerable theme and, much as I detest and deplore the breaking of nations, for me it is even fascinating to accompany in imagination the fighting-men of the past, whether I do so in the writings of Mottram or Sassoon, of Wellington or the Elizabethan dramatists. To many younger spirits, war does not naturally exist; its occurrence hitherto has been too ridiculous to be worth the expense of reason; its excitement has been insanely crude, its purposes piratical, its effects disgraceful, its habits murderous. The knell of war has been rung, if I perceive rightly what is in the consciousness of the coming race, by mere obsolescence, rather than through the arguments of experience. To me, again, the fact of books and reading is gloriously easy; the place in which I live is largely built of authors, great and little, whose pages I turn and revive by second nature. But sometimes, what have our bookshelves to say to us, who are by inheritance and inclination readers? Nothing, or something blurred; and we have a temporary sense of a world of men which might not need nor resort to the library for recreation or profounder tuition; which might look on a folio of a thousand ink-burdened pages bound in the hide of an animal as being just as appropriate to a dwelling as a stuffed elephant. Even omnibus volumes would be to them a fantastic toy. Their minds would collect what they approve by less cumbrous machinery.

Meanwhile, we are most of us believers in the method and benefit of what we know as literature; we give our hearts to personalities who have excelled in the creation of character, incident,

attitude and style; we admit without misgiving a
marvellous enchantment in vast designs, or
partial expressions, by the heroes of the age of
prose and verse. We too endeavour to represent
our conquest of our circumstances in words, and
are romantic enough to think that it matters.
I have met Englishmen, and strong ones too,
who are as much concerned over the uncertainty
of our poetry as of our pound. It is not then
mere sentiment or academic opportunism, I
fancy, which has induced me to offer, in accepting
the difficult honour of one year's Clark Lectures,
a study of an Englishman who perhaps more
than any of his contemporaries understood alike
the poetry and the pound, and the two worlds in
which our race has believed itself to have
travelled until now. And in naming Charles
Lamb with regard to the romantic stage of the
world's development I have an under-plot: I have
formed a notion that he begins to be neglected.
We have been informed by some critics that
Lamb thought "King Lear" a play unfit for stage
representation because he never saw Shakespeare's version acted, and so, poor Lamb, he
could not judge; a late ardent biographer has
thought him an inferior judge of poetry because
he had the simplicity to delight in "Isabella",
by Keats; an essayist of ingenuity nearest to

Elia's among us has included Lamb among his instances of shallower imaginative draught. Perhaps I should not commit an injustice if I said that Lamb is frequently fobbed off as a contemporary of Wordsworth and of Keats who liked roast pig, puns, dogs'-eared books, whist, artificial language, writing for magazines, quotations and parodies; who disliked churches, Goethe, the Lake District, philosophy, punctuality, Shelley's voice, sanity, Scots, Jews and schoolmasters. If it is so, it is not surprising; for nobody has been more ingenious in professing unimportance than Lamb, except Lear's Fool.

Nobody has been less inclined to exemplify in his course and habits the romantic character. To Lamb, the phrase which we conveniently use every day of "the Romantic Movement" must have been especially tedious and probably without point. The proposition that he himself was a part of that progress of feeling would have been alarming, and reprehensible in a jest. Remembering that, I shall try not to labour my portrait of him and my chart of his imaginative action, but rather let them take shape as I go, only declaring at once what I see in him: the splendid range of his veiled mind, the freedom of his sympathies, his command of human experience and his intuitive adventures in the visionary or abstract. The beginning of this matter must be an allusion to the period into which Lamb was born, and the conditions under which he began to grow—a period and conditions which it would not be easy to parallel in the England that we have now, and are apparently doomed never again to be echoed or reflected.

The second half of the eighteenth century in England proceeded past the date of Lamb's birth—1775—without violent change of form; solid excellence, classical ornament, ceremonious behaviour, shapely argument, contemplative patience, individuality of manners, distinction of ranks and callings, and over all an accomplished art of life prevailed. One would not enter into a comparative estimate of that state of civilization and our own, or try to measure all the good and evil then—on being quite sure what the terms stand for—with our advanced possibilities. You may say we travel faster—but they took their ease at their inn. But, apart from certain very dangerous deep holes, the period offered a good surface. Common necessities were readily obtained, employment was steady, the public interests were little polluted, the stage, the press, the church were maintained at a standard of strength and candour by a general keenness of taste. Bad plays were hissed off, bad

authors written off. Moreover the town (in spite
of Cowper) had not dispirited and depopulated
the country. I detect no pervading artificiality
of mind at that period. The squire might build a
sham ruin, the Cit might fit out his country box
with a Chinese temple, a Chatterton might earn
a few shillings by supplying a pewterer with
forged mediaeval family papers; but that is not
the kind of artificiality I am touching upon. What
a man knew in England in 1775, he could swear
to; and what he did not know he left alone. (Let
me admit, of course, the exception of politics,
recalling the sentence of the elder Pitt in that
very year, "There is hardly a man in our streets,
though so poor as hardly to be able to get his
daily bread, but thinks he is the legislator of
America".) In intellectual affairs, we had not
yet acquired the knack of light-hearted equality.
"I've read your stuff" was not, then, a com-
plimentary mode of address to an author from
one just able to write his name. There was no
hurry to obtain autographs for unopened copies
of "The Traveller" or "A Sentimental Journey";
but those works were read and re-read. Within
narrower limits, there was soundness; and the
embarrassment of being required by social custom to show an ardour over a wandering variety
of topics had not arisen—the embarrassment of

having missed the latest novel or Miss Z's
opinion of it, or mistaking a mention of Mr
Epstein for a reference to film production.

My remarks have led towards the literary
stability of England about 1775 partly in order
that I might introduce Charles Lamb's father,
a steady clerk, who was at that time producing
a little book of his own verses for the amusement
of a Friendly Society to which he belonged. The
Society met at the Devil Tavern to discuss their
benevolent work; a bust of Apollo adorned their
dining-room; and (verse being regarded as a
pleasant, intelligible way of writing) John Lamb
was for a few years their laureate. His dog's
name was Prior, in honour of a favourite author;
he was also a lover of "Hudibras". No more
than this; details are few; but do we not see the
plain honesty of such a character and his circle?
We find John Lamb the elder, too, at the theatre,
watching Garrick in performance after performance with anxious and admiring comparison;
"greatest, he would say, in Bayes". And at the
theatre we find with him a godfather of his
famous son—Francis Fielde, an oilman whose
shop was in Holborn. It was sufficient reward
for Fielde, who supplied the illumination of the
"orchestra and various avenues" of Drury Lane
Theatre for years, to receive free admission from

Palmer the comedian or from Sheridan. I shall
not say that such oilmen are not to be found
nowadays; I merely point out that such earnest
Londoners characterize the period we are glancing
at. They were ordinary citizens, but they were
careful in their valuations of life, in subdivisions
not illustrating a complex consciousness but an
ordered thoughtfulness.

Into this period of firm merits and unboastful
attainments there entered the spirit of discovery,
one of its aspects being the geographical. James
Cook seeking a southern continent, Bruce track-
ing the sources of the Nile, were not merely
treated as news of a day. The spacious publications of their narratives did not pass rapidly,
as comfortable excitements with a suggestion
of ideal summer holidays, through the circulating libraries. They deeply affected and en-
larged the minds of the generation that soon
afterwards welcomed a series of Odysseys from
other heroes; the presence of their fortitude,
the picture of their unknown regions added a
grandeur to the fireside conversations of many
years. And yet, the age of legend was not extinct.
The wonders of the world were still to be reported
in full. The youth who saw the sea for the first
time then, his mind haunted with what he had
read and heard, was not limited to speculations

on the differences of luxury between one liner and the next. He thought (or so Lamb says) "of the great deep, and of those who go down into it; of its thousand isles, and of the vast continents it washes; of its receiving the mighty Plata, or Orellana, into its bosom, without disturbance, or sense of augmentation; of Biscay swells, and the mariner

> For many a day, and many a dreadful night,
> Incessant labouring round the stormy Cape;

of fatal rocks, and the 'still-vexed Bermoothes'; of great whirlpools, and the water-spout; of sunken ships, and sumless treasures swallowed up in the unrestoring depths: of fishes and quaint monsters, to which all that is terrible on·earth—

> Be but as buggs to frighten babes withal,
> Compared with the creatures in the sea's entral;

of naked savages, and Juan Fernandez; of pearls, and shells; of coral beds, and of enchanted isles; of mermaids' grots".

Not unlucky in the characteristics of the times to which he came, the child Charles Lamb was surely fortunate in his precise environment. His earliest home was the Temple, to this day a beautiful seclusion in the great town, a green and sunny glade (on auspicious visits); "its church, its halls, its gardens, its fountain, its river", he·

says, were his early world. Here, the winged
horse that guarded the Inner Temple-hall, the
frescoes of the Virtues on Paper Buildings (his
"first hint of allegory"), the sun-dials with
their inscriptions and stealing "dark lines", the
grotesque heads round the church, became the
property of his fancy; but more so, those Benchers
who, in strong individuality of costume, gesture
and humour walked the terrace, and who are
still lively in an Essay of Elia. These men were
of a make that, even in the sheltered avenues of
the law, is gone. They made up, for the child
Lamb, "the mythology of the Temple", and
coalesced in his "innocent superstition" with
the majestic supermen of the Old Testament.
The mention of the Old Testament takes us into
Crown Office Row and the library of one of the
Benchers—Samuel Salt, under whose roof lived
the Lambs as his housekeepers. Here Charles,
like his sister Mary, was made acquainted with
old books in plenty; over and above his father's
miscellaneous collection. Lamb himself has expressed the vitality of such an education as
the freedom of "good old English reading", a
roomfull of it, gives a child; he has dwelt upon
the error of explaining too coolly to the young-
ster whatever puzzles him. It was his chance, at
any rate, to meet with such masterpieces of

simple romance as the "Pilgrim's Progress", "Compleat Angler", and "Parables of Our Lord" by himself, in the season of his readiest impressibility; then there were more extravagant productions, as, Salmon's "Modern History" (the repertory whence the poet Collins drew oriental hints for his young verse), Glanvill's "Considerations Touching Witches", and Stackhouse's "New History of the Holy Bible" with its prodigious engravings. Such a book as the last, merely as an object in one's neighbourhood, might well seem a relic of some mightier race—a Pyramid of authorship. Taking his pleasures with a child's seriousness, Charles was soon able to add a new province to his kingdom; he has told us of the rich scripture-truth which his first play (at Drury Lane, when he was five years old) imparted to him. Out of Salmon's History, he had brought some picture of Persepolis, but here in the opera "Artaxerxes" he "was in Persepolis". He had seen in Rowe's "Shakespeare" an engraving of a tent scene, and even that was glorified into the curtain which at length concealed the gorgeous demi-gods.

This boy of waking dreams, who could not see a chimney-sweep emerging from his dismal ascent to wave his triumphant brush aloft without thinking of the third apparition in "Macbeth", was not denied some acquaintance with country life at this juncture. Here we may wonder what the decline of genuine rural affairs and intimacies will do with the sensibilities of the future. It will hardly bring into being richer memories, more delicate understandings, more gracious desires and fancies. Lamb enjoyed a kind of double benefice; his country childhood was spent, part in the great house and grounds, part in the farmhouse and its tenements. These entertainments he owed to his mother's family in Hertfordshire. It is observable that he derived less of distinct memory from the farmhouse, Mackery End, than from the hall of Blakesware, which sheltered the genius of antiquity and secrecy. Lamb never became a good farmer or field naturalist, but he adopted Blakesware with a rapture. Such houses and their treasures are fast disappearing, and Lamb himself lived to see the ruins of this one, which only brought back to him more intensely the relation between the child and the tapestries—"all Ovid on the walls"; the miraculous for ever enacting; the twelve Caesars in marble, "in the coldness of death, yet freshness of immortality"; the portrait gallery, that seemed "ready to speak"; the haunted room, the hall of justice, and judgment chair. And out of doors there was even sweeter invitation to worship the glory of the ancient time, where high and fruitful walls shut in the little paradise, and formal terraces and their ornaments rose like a stage for a masque; beyond lay a region of remoter time, a firry wilderness whose midmost statue assured the child of Pan or Silvanus, commanding his innocent idolatry; and a lake glistened between the trees, farther off, just beyond his privileges, like some half-discovered inland sea in the old geographers.

But the time came for Lamb's return to London, and to his early schools. The first of his teachers was Miss Chambers, who had been acquainted with Goldsmith—not long since laid in his grave in the Temple. Lamb passed presently to an Academy kept by Mr William Bird in the neighbourhood of Bartlett's Buildings (parts of which stand as he saw them then). This Academy, of course immeasurably inferior in educational theory to modern schools, deserves some commendation; for it at least gave Lamb, besides a handwriting and some other plain equipment, "a world of little associated circumstances", a strain of queer music throughout life. The schoolmaster wore a flowered Indian gown, which improved his awe-striking eminence; the figures on it, the pupils "used to inter-

pret into hieroglyphics of pain and suffering".
So much the greater the bliss, when this high
priest presented to Lamb the prize for best
spelling. We may sum up the Academy as, like
all of its kind, a mixture of the prosaic and the
romantic, the useful and the delightful, and for-
mative without formality.

Lamb's brother John—almost twelve years
older—had had his principal education in Christ's
Hospital, and by following him there in the year
1782 Charles only continued in that double relation to the practical and the mysterious which
had hitherto been allotted to him. The Hospital
at that date stood unremoved in Newgate Street,
and not only was it venerable itself in the dignity
of two centuries, but it preserved the lineaments
of the more ancient Grey Friars. It was largely
monastic in its life, which was mainly cloistered
away from the town. If we consider to the full
the traditional words, "the religious, royal, and
ancient foundation of Christ's Hospital", and
especially if we allow in the word "religious"
a tinge of the old Virgilian sense of "religio",
we obtain a good impression of what it meant
to a perceptive child to become a part of that
strange school. He was officially "a poor
orphan"; but he saw that the powers that were
had set him in this grand fabric of authority,

learning, munificence and high ceremony. His "very garb", as Lamb said, gave him at once pride and restraint. He ate his meals, and read his books, under the painted gaze of his benefactors; before he left the school, he was aware that the world's merchants in the City had their eyes on youths like himself for the future of their houses. His schoolmasters were a class apart, rather after the manner of fellows of colleges; their function was to promote the arts and sciences; nearly all of them were Blues, perfect in the spirit of the school. The humbler stewardship and government were in other hands. Part of it was allotted to the boys themselves according to their rank.

Above all, the grand invention of organized games being as yet distant, it was possible for those boys to recreate their minds inventively; and, in such mediaeval surroundings and amid the series of curious or splendid occasions that belonged to the Hospital's calendar, it is not odd that "a turn for romance above most other boys" characterized them. In that school, charms were still in use; there were mysterious words in the vocabulary; and we are told by others than Lamb of romantic customs. For example, at night, the Fazzer walked, or, as the phrase was, he "was out". He was a goblin, though in fact only one of the big boys, but invested with the attributes of a mischievous demon, "our elf, our spectre, our Flibbertigibbet, 'who put knives in our pillows and halters in our pews'". Then, while all dormitories produce their tale-tellers, here the kind of tale was much the same year after year—some marvel of genii, fairies, witches and knights and ladies. Lamb records "the peculiar avidity with which such books as the "Arabian Nights' Entertainments" and others of a still wilder cast were sought for by the boys", and he mentions a local romance which is well worth finding, "The Fortunate Bluecoat Boy". It was in the nature of a legend, showing with profuse historical detail how once a wealthy young widow had fallen in love with a Blue and married him to her equally desirable person and fortune. It kept alive, like some other fables, the idea of a Golden Age of those "cloisters pale". On certain days, the boys were sent out of the school for "whole-day leaves", and then they were apt to travel in the light of their day-dreams. Lamb gives the pleasant glimpse of one little band "setting off, without map, card or compass, on a serious expedition to find out *Philip Quarll's Island*"; and he appears to have been himself the leading spirit in a similar enter-prise. "Fired with a perusal of the Abyssinian

Pilgrim's exploratory ramblings after the cradle of the infant Nilus", he went off at summer sunrise to trace the New River to its source in distant Hertfordshire.

About the figures of the principal masters and officers of the Hospital, a serio-comic atmosphere clung. Chief of these was James Boyer, himself a daylight Fazzer—a plain schoolmaster, or an ogre. To Charles Lamb particularly, who was gently used by master and boy alike throughout his schooldays—he affects that this mildness was due to his access to a governor in his own home —Boyer was a subject for half-amused observation, and the element of comedy was the richer because of the artful difference maintained by Boyer from his colleague Matthew Field. In one long schoolroom these classical masters divided empire. Boyer had all the thunders of the scene; Field looked in occasionally and, finding his boys still there, heard a little grammar and left them to their "mirth and uproar". Boyer, not authorized to interfere with the methods of this gentlemanly divine, contrived to make ironical use of them in his didactical talks with his "pale students"; if we are to credit Coleridge's repeated encomiums, these talks were valuable expositions of the genuine and the false in literature. From some specimens that

remain of Boyer's own verses, which Lamb calls
"crampt to barbarism", one may see that he
would not care much for flowers of speech.
Boyer had a keen eye for the boy of promise; and
he did not miss Charles Lamb. He ordered him
to copy into his book, the Liber Aureus, one of his
exercises in English verse; and it is thought
he regretted that an impediment of speech prevented Lamb from moving up into his form of
Grecians and proceeding with the Hospital's aid
to a University. One other master stood out in
the school—and in Lamb's mind: he was a mathe-
matician named Wales, and his nautical wit and
force, and his former voyages with Captain
Cook, made him one of Lamb's memories.[1]

What, it will be asked, did a boy learn in the
Grammar School of Christ's Hospital? Lamb's
writings supply an answer (even if we skip
that Latin letter to Coleridge declaring that
he was stuffed with learning from top to
bottom, as by a surgical operation). He acquired
a very useful knowledge of Latin, and an intelligent notion of Greek—alike the languages
and the literatures. He was accustomed to the
clear statement of his thoughts in English, prose

[1] And Coleridge's. See "The Friend," 1818, ii,
72–3, for his eulogy of a pamphlet by "my old mathematical master, a man of an uncommonly clear head."

and verse, and the thoroughness of the times demanded not only arranged ideas but good writing and spelling. He became a practical arithmetician. Upon the information, and ability to handle it, which Lamb brought away from Christ's Hospital at the age of fourteen, were founded a career by no means inefficient or irregular in the East India House, and an inimitable style in essays and in letters largely consisting in abundant dexterous allusion to classical literature and example, but more deeply in an unerring sense of balanced prose. There is another instance immediately appropriate. John Lamb also left the Hospital at about the same age, and with similar grounding; he wrote eloquently, was a capital critic of art and literature, and held the post of Accountant at the South Sea House. In the writings of Charles and John Lamb alike, there is much imaginative recourse to an educational treasury since less familiar—the Bible. The Bluecoat boys heard the Testaments read and re-read, and perhaps some of the iron entered into their soul; but did they not insensibly gain a strength of judgment, of illustration, of vocabulary and of prose impact which could hardly be won from other sources? Possibly the literary pilgrim in England would not waste his enthusiasm by visiting

Christ Church, Newgate Street, as one of the creative scenes in our Romantic prose and poetry.

The name of Coleridge has already slipped in. Whatever systems humanity may set up, personal contacts are the great thing. The son of the dreamy Devonshire clergyman, and the son of the joke-scattering private servant in the Temple met as Bluecoat boys, to form a friendship of half a century; and though we have not much exact account of their school companionship, we know its kind. Here Coleridge, the rapid conqueror of all learning actual or abstract, in "deep and sweet intonations" interpreting to the world of Christ's Hospital playgrounds his mystical philosophers; there Lamb, listening, deferential, intelligent, his angel captured,—yet not so rapt as his partner; observing with a smile the effect of the astonishing young logician, metaphysician and bard upon "the casual passer through the Cloisters". Other children of that beautiful and now pathetic microcosm come into the group. There Charles Valentine Le Grice ever challenges Coleridge by virtue of his own nimble improvisation—not destined to mature into more than a handful of occasional pamphlets; Bob Allen hungrily expects the "poignant jests" of these heroes, half-aware of his own fate, which was to become a newspaper hack. Whoever comes, we are already aware of Lamb, "not so clever yet much cleverer", the real romantic among them, seeing them all as a clan of immortals—but not forgetting the time and the fact that his aunt Hetty is about to arrive with her useful parcels.

There was not in that school under the rod of Boyer any measurable intention of supplying new blood to the cause of English literature. Indeed, the authorities were not well aware that there was such a cause; and I am reminded of a public report on the school's exhibitioners at a much later date, in which it is written: "Some have died, and some have gone into literature; but few have failed to do other than well". Yet the remarkable position is that Christ's Hospital, during the last two decades of the eighteenth century, produced a large number of men who in one way or another contributed to the literature of their day—some of them did more. Besides Coleridge, Lamb, Leigh Hunt, and the others noticed, let me briefly introduce some names now little known: John Mathew Gutch, the Bristol journalist who published special editions of Coleridge and edited or collected a variety of old poets, such as George Wither and Herrick; George Richards, whose Oxford prize-poem delighted Byron so well; William Pitt

Scargill, a novelist, whose short sketches helped
to establish the now fallen *Athenaeum* journal;
T. S. Surr, another novelist and in his day
a favourite; T. H. Horne, a mighty miscellaneous
writer, but among the fathers of the British
Museum Reading Room; Jem White, the gay
deviser of "Original Letters of Sir John Falstaff";
Thomas Mitchell, translator of Aristophanes, a
Quarterly reviewer; Thomas Barnes, a brilliant
critic for *The Examiner* and a constructive editor
of *The Times*. The list could be considerably
extended, but these are sufficient examples of
the enthusiasm for modern writing which per-
vaded the school of Elia at his epoch. To what,
or whom, is this paradoxical effulgence to be
ascribed? To Dr Johnson, who was seen, before
Lamb could know Johnson from Boswell, visiting
his protégé in the Cloisters? To Lamb's George
Dyer (historian of Cambridge University), re-
visiting the scenes of his first poetical perambu-
lations? To the circulating libraries in Newgate
Street? To that fine old expression the Romantic
Movement—

> For not through eastern windows only
> When daylight comes, comes in the light—

making way through the perfect phalanx of
sound divinity and Terence and Xenophon? To

the laconic Boyer at his end of the Grammar
School, reading out the parliamentary debates or
"taking Shakespeare" by way of interlude? To
Field at the other end, ignoring the copies of
"Peter Wilkins" and "Arabian Nights" that
crowded Phaedrus and Spence off the inky desks?
To Charles Lamb perhaps, bringing in from the
book-cupboard of his father or the more heavily
moroccoed cabinets of his governor a hundred
sly references and tempting suggestions of the
English world of books?

Let me reduce the vagueness of that last
question. Lamb might have read some unexpected authors—a Cowley kept him quiet in the
window-seat at Blakesware at the age of six or
so—but he did not emerge from school as an
antiquary in books. The verses that are preserved in Boyer's write-in book are regular
eighteenth-century work, a little strengthened,
I should say, by Boyer's injunctions to write
with the good sense of Homer; there are reminiscences of Thomas Gray in them. If we
consult the earliest letters of Lamb that are so
far known, being of a much later date than his
schooldays, they show that his reading until his
early manhood had been principally in the
eighteenth-century poets, from Parnell to Mac-
pherson's Ossian, and we may be surprised

when he speaks of such Elian authors as Quarles, Wither, Jeremy Taylor, and Fairfax the translator of Tasso as not having come his way yet.

Lamb has left two papers on his old school, which must both be considered in connection with their occasion and object. The first, called "Recollections of Christ's Hospital", appeared in that foundered ark of conservative emotions, the Gentleman's Magazine. This magazine was not normally in Lamb's first thoughts, but, being a good judge of the sorts of periodicals and their audiences, when some attacks on the control of the school were being made in Radical quarters, he saw where he might best lend his aid to the defence. This was in 1813. The "Recollections" labour a little, for Lamb conveyed them in the serious, judicious manner expected by his readers of the occasion; besides, he was, and he knew he was, presenting a case. He was not going to greater extent of confession and complaint than was called for by the opposition and the point at issue. But far be it from me to hint that the "Recollections" distorted his personal attitude towards his fostering-place. "For me", he wrote, "I do not know whether a constitutional imbecility"—a Gentlemanly Latinism, not an allusion to family secrets—"does not incline me too obstinately to cling to the remembrances of childhood; in an inverted ratio to the usual sentiments of mankind, nothing that I have been engaged in since seems of any value or importance, compared to the colours which imagination gave to everything then". And so he spoke his timely word for the school as a "body corporate", a monument of benevolent reason.

Seven years later he had quite another occasion and indeed another theme. He had by that time invented his disguise of "Elia", under which he need not be Charles Lamb of the India House; and while still the honour of his school is implicit in the essay "Christ's Hospital Five and Thirty Years Ago", that essay deliberately parts from the experiences of Charles Lamb as a schoolboy and utters the feelings of those less fortunate. "I was a poor friendless boy"—a Shakespearean transference of sympathies, for which perhaps conversations with Coleridge had provided an impulse—the contrast with all his own advantages. With how keen a sensuousness did Elia in that page cause the very tea and hot rolls that Lamb had had of a morning to seem outrageous luxury, and the hunk of common *crug* and small leather-flavoured beer of the unprivileged to be so much the more wretched? But the antithesis was not complete. Elia admitted that the child Lamb, when his relative unfolded for him in the

cloister her daily treat of a hot dinner, had some
difficulty in falling to, "a troubling over-con-
sciousness", a "sympathy for those who were
too many to share in it". In other touches, too,
we recognize in Lamb at school an imaginative
insight into the sufferings and the perplexities
of his mates,—part of that wonderful fineness of
vision which also gave him then, as he turned his
illustrated British Novelists, a world of friends
as though they were to be met in the street:

Clarissa mournful, and prim Grandison!
All Fielding's, Smollett's heroes rose to view;
I saw, and I believed the phantoms true.
But, above all, that most romantic tale
Did o'er my raw credulity prevail
Where Glums and Gawries wear mysterious things,
That serve at once for jackets and for wings.

If in these annotations I appear to be em-
phasizing Lamb as a unique being and his childhood as an isolated thing of beauty, I am sorry;
for there is nothing that divided him in his early
responsiveness from many and many a child.
Rather I would show him in his elements and
his external associations as typical, with this
distinction, answerable to his manhood as well;
that he had ordinary qualities in their most
lively and delightful degrees. Mr Lucas, whose
work for Lamb has never been over-praised,

and cannot be, once described him as a "pocket Shakespeare", and that word condenses my meaning. Lamb himself had a way of thinking that in one point he was out of the ordinary. I have quoted his words of 1813, on his valuing his boyhood "in an inverted ratio to the usual sentiments of mankind"; others of ten years later are more often recalled, where he affects to characterize "the late Elia": "He was too much of the boy-man. The *toga virilis* never sate gracefully on his shoulders. The impressions of infancy had burnt into him, and he resented the impertinence of manhood. These were weaknesses; but such as they were, they are a key to explicate some of his writings". As for weaknesses, let the chivalrous and influential life of Lamb as a whole be thought over. The key is worth a word. When we consider that (for example) Lamb wrote the first study of Hogarth's genius in which that genius was understood as being far above mere burlesque, and that in this radiant criticism Lamb was only exploring with his mature powers "the manner in which Hogarth's prints used to affect me" on the walls of Blakesware as one of his "noblest enjoyments" of contemplation, this key is felt to have something almost magic in it. It connects, rather than explicates; it combines periods in one room; we see a boy-man at once conceiving and fulfilling an original and a secure work of appreciative truth, things indeed

> to babes revealed
> Which were from the wise concealed.

Do we then do well nowadays in our frequent insistence on a sort of hygienic and suspiciously graduated education, our safeguarding children's minds from any possible struggle with the intellectual interests of their elders and their own solutions? Well or ill, the world has changed; the future is to be still neater, still compacter, still narrower, still safer from fancy; and it is only the vestigial eye of the romantic with which we are now looking back to—an eighteenth-century childhood.

I have endeavoured, from the fragmentary passages of evidence that survive a century and a half, in a more fragmentary way to revive Lamb's infancy in the Temple, with the restraint and liberty that it afforded, nourishers of a "serious and affectionate" consciousness; whence grew a high humility, a sensible acceptance of limitations of place and power, an unpretentious habit of transforming the things of the sense into those of the imagination, a union of the temporary with the perpetual. Prophetic years they were of the approaching middle age which gave us, not such fantasies as Spenser, nor celestial thoughts with Shelley, but the town pavement or the card table and those who possessed them, spirited away from the common clutch of mortality—tenderest, ethereal-lighted conversation pieces. And in this ripening of a vital faculty, it has been signified that the solitary summer hours in a half-deserted mansion, with the little boy left to converse with the clocks indoors and the orange-trees in the gardens, had their conspicuous share. Of schools and schoolmasters something has been recollected—of their dignity, their picturesque simplicity, their challenge to the wit, the fancy and vigour of youth, their steady exact instruction, their suggestions of a world worth conquering beyond their doors and boundaries. Of friendships and the attractive variety of friends, of fascinating talents and achievements, the sketch has included a trace; a pity that no more than a trace of Coleridge's first dawning on Lamb's inward sight (outward too, but that is all one) can be made out. This sigh, it happens, is my cue for resuming, and shortly concluding, the narrative which winds through the first stage of this study.

In the year 1789, Lamb, aged fourteen, had risen without difficulty to the class of Deputy

Grecians in his school. He had read at least his
Virgil, Sallust, Terence, selections from Lucian,
and Xenophon; his compositions were acknow-
ledged to prove his unusual handiness with the
Latin language, and his general aptitude for a
classical career. The upper grammar master, who
had not long before rescued Coleridge from a
self-sought apprenticeship to a shoemaker and
was industriously handling him for his next steps
in church or state, had also selected Lamb as a
boy who might proceed.—But Lamb stammered,
and the chances against his being successful in
the duties of the clergy appeared too great; he
was therefore not advanced to the rank of
Grecian, and entered on his last days at school
in that disappointment. His principal com-
panions had gone or were going, safe with their
exhibitions, to the Universities; and at that date
there was more of rarity and romance in that by
far, for a "half-starved Bluecoat boy" at least,
than there is now. For Lamb, instead of this
imaginative reward, there lay ahead a desert,
as many would think, of "dry drudgery at the
desk's dead wood". It is recorded that he submitted to this situation "without a murmur";
and only indirectly, in the main, do we receive
from his essays and his verses the force of his
regret. One word from "Oxford in the Vaca-

tion" whimsically confesses it: "such a one as myself, who has been *defrauded* in his young years of the sweet food of academic institution". But his genial resolution of turning his condition into idealizations did not fail him in this matter; for he adopted the Universities, both of them, as metaphysically his, and here in Cambridge especially he could come in later years;

> Yet can I fancy, wandering 'mid thy towers,
> Myself a nursling, Granta, of thy lap;
> My brow seems tightening with the Doctor's cap,
> And I walk *gownéd*; feel unusual powers.

I must add the next line:

> Strange forms of logic clothe my admiring speech.

Leaving school, then, at the end of 1789, ready to be turned into a good Clerk, Lamb left childhood behind as a division of time, and maybe now more than later seemed prospective and citizen-like. There was one experience above the rest which demonstrated his seniority. We accompanied him to his first play; since then, the rules of Christ's Hospital, which I understand are now modified, inhibiting all play-going, had caused "that old Artaxerxes evening" tantalizingly to "ring in his fancy". In his town-clothes, he quickly attempted to renew his Delectable Theatre. "I expected", he says, "the same feelings to come again with the same occasion." In vain: "I had left the temple a devotee, and was returned a rationalist. The same things were there materially; but the emblem, the reference, was gone". Green baize was green baize, the prompter (no fairy hand) rang his own bell, a machine elevated the orchestra lights, "the actors were men and women painted". The saddened boy walked home from "an indifferent comedy"; not long afterwards he ventured afresh, and saw Mrs Siddons in "Isabella". About the years 1790 and 1791, his fifteenth and sixteenth years, he contrived to be a valuable patron of the two-shilling gallery; and on this circumstance it has depended that we have for ever his living pictures of "Some of the Old Actors", restored from the shadows by him at the prompting of an old playbill thirty-two years after. Those copious delineations, exquisite discriminations prove that with Lamb, when one enchantment had run its course, another was not wanting; the deep sweet fervours of the child's wonder did not yield to elder coldness or an altered morality; the transition from the imperfect material and "ignorant present" to perfect illusion and comprehending timelessness, the grace of his childhood, did not "die all" as he undertook the business of manhood.

CHAPTER II

THE NEW POETRY

If it seems acceptable that until the year 1789 the upbringing of Lamb was contributory to a poetic character, it is a little hard to see his situation that year and for some time afterwards in the same light. A precious vision of the world of thought and imagination which should be made his own had been taken from him; and instead of the Coleridgean paths which he pictured, his daily round was very quickly defined for him—in an office. We know fairly well what was said on this occasion by his patrons, who were only doing their best. Thomas Coventry, the most formidable of Elia's "Old Benchers", and the richest, said one day to a merchant named Joseph Paice[1], "There is a lad

---

[1] Paice may have been of greater importance in Lamb's life than is disclosed. Anne Manning ("Family Pictures," 1861), with her old relative's papers before her, writes of his "refined and poetical taste," and says that "his memory was stored, with poetic treasures of the Elizabethan era, for which he manifested even a religious reverence." He was a great friend of

whom I placed some years since in the Blue Coat School, now on the point of leaving it, and I know not what to do with him"; Paice, under Coventry a director of the South Sea Company, replied, "Let him have the run of my counting-house till something better offers". Both gentlemen were aware that Lamb's brother was steadily advancing in the South Sea House, and surely, with warm Pickwickian anticipations, had a notion that something better would offer there for Charles also.

About this time Lamb was excited in a boyish way by the French Revolution, but he made no objection to going into Joseph Paice's office, and there learned the routine; there, he says, he gained for life "whatever there is of the man of business in my composition", and it is too easy a habit to smile at Lamb's modicum of effectiveness in business. But he gained something more —the example of a beautiful courtesy, which appeared in all his employer's actions. He had, in his restriction, a constant symbol of romance, and the merchant of Bread Street Hill became in his fancy a "Sir Calidore, or Sir Tristan". In 1791 Lamb passed on to the South Sea House, Samuel Richardson and other writers. I have a copy of Joseph Hall's "Contemplations," 1679, with his name in it.

where he was not destined to stay long, but where
he added richly to his treasures of perception in
the human scene. The first of Elia's essays was
to be only a delicate revival of the place and its
people, the shade and the shadows, as he discovered them in the dreaming world of 1791.
I say "he discovered them", but there is a
mixture of subtlety in the essay, a quibble here
and there for the severe historian; probably we
have in this the faculty of Lamb for creating
complete verisimilitude out of experiences not
his own, the "fantastic shapes" that his elder
brother's reminiscences at home had prepared
for him at the South Sea House when he arrived,
superimposed on the "living accountants". In
any event, there is no denying the sweet influence of an office where every fortnight the
deputy-accomptant's rooms resounded to a con-
cert, at his own expense; where the deputy-
secretary was a "polished man of letters", great
as an epigrammatist in the corners of the newspapers; where, in short, almost all the clerks
"had arrived at considerable proficiency on the
German flute".

The South Sea House was already an antiquity
rather than an instrument for the coming generation; and early in 1792 Lamb was transplanted,
still under the care of an Old Bencher, his actual

school-governor, Samuel Salt. How excellent looks that patriarchal system wherever we may view the circumstances of its working! What a fund of meaning then in that word "governor"! Dare I even introduce a word of regret that Keats did not permit Mr Abbey the wholesale merchant to make a comfortable nook for him in the department of Tea? Meanwhile, under the guarantees of simple good old men whose poetry Mr Pope had supplied in far greater quantities than they would ever exhaust, our romantic Lamb is awarded a not disgraceful security for life in the East India House. Even at this valuable opportunity, we should do a great injustice to him if we suppose acceptance to have been a simple matter of the main chance. Warmed with auguries of his future fortune, the youth nevertheless faces the immediate prospect of three years without receipt of a salary. Then, more deeply, he compares the seldom mitigated confinement ahead of him with recent freedom, and above all—for Mr Lucas's deduction seems the true one—with early spring in the Hertfordshire meadows and an awakening love for one now to be parted from him as though by some dreary sea. Other considerations—his duties, as he and his age received the matter, to his old home, now menaced by change and decline

—overcome even these; and Lamb becomes for his time and for all time a clerk of the India House.

One leaves him finding his way among the ledgers awhile in order to enquire what was happening in the world of poetry, some rumours of which had stirred him before he left school. The time was a peculiar one in its divergence from recent moods of verse. Not long before, satire had seemed the representative expression; Churchill had "blazed the comet of a season" with his fierce succession of couplets, and his angry wit had been indulged at the expense of his better genius. Even Cowper, in 1782, began his public course as poet with satires; Chatterton, apart from his Rowley poems, had calculated that his chance of temporary success lay in his producing lampoons "more to embroil the fray". Numerous reprints rewarded the authors of that unamusing medley "The Rolliad"; and when the Reverend William Mason, instead of "Odes" or an "English Garden" in gray blank verse, put forth his share of castigatory couplets, he did not lose his fee. The solemn applicant from East Anglia, George Crabbe, in the ten years ending 1785, contributed to this warfare, not unnoticed, a mighty militia of united aphorisms and comments on manners. There is a collection of ten volumes—Debrett's "New Foundling

Hospital for Wit" and "Asylum for Wit"—
completed in 1793, which records beyond mistake the spirit of the Muses during a large part of
the period of Lamb's early life. I shall not be so
melodramatic as to conjure all this tradition of
coffee-house brilliance out of the scene by waving
a copy of the "Lyrical Ballads" at the wits. Men
like Matthias, Hayley, Byron, Moore, Luttrell,
Sam Rogers, "the sneering Smiths", not to mention Crabbe again returning to metropolitan applause, besides a drove of neat immoral gentry
who always arrived with an "Iad" on any place
associated with liberal progress, maintained the
old-fashioned reader in his kind of verses and
verse interests until the day of Queen Victoria.

Yet beyond this regular dispensation of
obvious wisdom and metre, a new sentiment,
various in its intimations, was being considered
as the true source of poetry. The history of
this liberation of minds and feelings has been
sketched often and elaborately. In such a title
for a novel as "The Man of Feeling" (1771) connected with that of "The Minstrel, or The Progress of Genius" (completed in 1777) and
"Observations Relative Chiefly to Picturesque
Beauty on the Mountains and Lakes of Cumberland and Westmoreland" (1786) and "Solitude
considered with Respect to its Influence upon

the Mind and the Heart" (translated into English in 1791)—all examples of widely circulated
and contemplated books—we quickly refresh the
graciousness of the development; and the mention of a Rousseau with his "Social Contract"
or a Godwin with his "Political Justice", or a
series of titles like "The Rights of Man", "The
Rights of Woman", "The Rights of Animals"
and "The Rights of Nature against the Usur-
pation of Establishments", as quickly extends
the simple chart of romantic reform. This way
lay the invaluable madness of young intelligences
when Lamb began to look about him with the
curiosity of a just initiated contemporary.

In 1777 Dr Johnson had objected to the new
poetry, and the epigram which he attached to
Tom Warton's mantle ended, quite savagely,
with the word *Sonnet*. His indignation had not
been sufficient to repress this form of poetry,
then symptomatic of dangerous emotions. (At
the present moment, it is due to be revived and
made respectable once more.) Sonnets multiplied after 1777, and in that new fascination we
especially approach the chief figures of romantic
sensibility. Of many instances, one was prominent at the time, and is apt to my present
purpose. In Lamb's last year at school—1789—
a young man named William Lisle Bowles was

returning to Oxford a little inconvenienced by
the reflection that he owed some £70 for goods
supplied. Having spontaneously meditated a few
Sonnets, he paused in Bath to write them fair and
ask a printer named Cruttwell to make an offer
for them. Mr Cruttwell, a very fine printer,
at least offered to risk £5 of Bowles's in printing
"Fourteen Sonnets, Elegiac and Descriptive,
written during a Tour". Already our credulity
is strained, but more strain follows: Cruttwell
sold 500 copies, and asked for a new edition.
"Twenty-One Sonnets" came forth, another 500
copies were purchased; then 750 more, and—to
be brief—edition succeeded edition. One of the
early copies found its way to S. T. Coleridge,
in his blue clothes. What he read—if so light
and zephyrish a sensation could be called "reading"—captivated him so well that he tran-
scribed the Sonnets forty times, and made presents of the copies to his friends. There is no
choke-pear for us in having no actual record that
Lamb received one. His earliest letters show
his acquaintance with the Sonnets of Bowles,
and his community of pleasure in them with
Coleridge. In June 1796 he begins a letter by
praising one poem as sufficient to show the
poetic stability of the age "were there no such
beings extant as Burns and Bowles"; half-way

through the letter he marks one sonnet of a series as "that most exquisite and most Bowles-like of all".

It becomes necessary then that we should try to reanimate the beautiful as it appeared for a few years in the verse of Bowles to such gifted youths as Coleridge, Wordsworth, Southey and Lamb; and this is not usually thought an easy revival, for all those writers passed beyond the spell of the sonneteer, and so did the world in general, an age ago. The following was probably the best known of Bowles's pieces,—"The Bells, Ostend":

How sweet the tuneful bells' responsive peal!
　　As when, at opening morn, the fragrant breeze
　　Breathes on the trembling sense of wan disease,
So piercing to my heart their force I feel!
And hark! with lessening cadence now they fall!
　　And now, along the white and level tide,
　　They fling their melancholy music wide;
Bidding me many a tender thought recall
Of summer-days, and those delightful years
　　When by my native streams, in life's fair prime,
　　The mournful magic of their mingling chime
First waked my wondering childhood into tears!
But seeming now, when all those days are o'er,
The sounds of joy once heard, and heard no more.

What have we here? As yet, Tennyson was not, and the song of "Tears, idle tears" was far

in the future; meanwhile, Bowles discovered the
theme of a solitary and nervous grief, awakened
by an incidental experience of the utmost simplicity. He hymned a tender, sub-conscious unity
between the observer and the observed; the topic
was taken not because it might illustrate habits
of mankind but because to one man it was important, to the point of "magic". As yet, such
words as "magic", "melancholy", "chime"
had not been sicklied over by insensitive uses.
The first had not become an advertising counter,
the second was not associated with boarding-
houses or bank-balances, the third was still an
open-air music. And throughout this typical Sonnet, the clear touch upon a restricted vocabulary
was, and is, noteworthy. It is our way to strive
for effects in prose or verse by inventing the
most vociferous agglomerations of terms that
we can, and in the greatest possible number. Do
we lose sight of style? This minor poet Bowles,
in a poem of which the substance to us is insignificant perhaps or primitive, at least had
style; he understood how to make a background
of the tone suitable to his mind, and on that to
produce his more conspicuous expressions in a
proportion not detrimental to one another or the
sustaining basis. The same grace, the *simplex
munditiis*, haunted all through his Sonnets,

just as Mr Cruttwell's typography in its humbler part combined tranquillity with distinctness.

Let me now turn back to the young clerk in the East India House, a spirit of finer tone than the meditative Bowles, but receiving from him the encouragement of personal expression and of style. The year is 1794. Some years have passed since he was able to saunter in Hertfordshire, and the girl (whose phantasm gleams through Lamb's writings early and late) has been stolen away by time and geography— nothing uncommon, "aye, Madam, it is common". The little we know of Lamb's schooldays shows him inclined towards poetry; and from the year 1794 there survives fuller evidence that he would have won the poet's name. This is one of the sonnets of the thoughtful Londoner at the age of nineteen:

Was it some sweet Delight of Faery
That mocked my steps with many a lonely glade,
And fancied wanderings with a fair-hair'd maid?
Have these things been? or what rare witchery,
Impregning with delights the charméd air,
Enlighted up the semblance of a smile
In those fine eyes? methought they spake the while
Soft soothing things, which might enforce despair
To drop the murdering knife, and let go by
His foul resolve. And does the lonely glade

Still court the foot-steps of the fair-hair'd maid?
Still in her locks the gales of summer sigh?
While I forlorn do wander heedless where,
And 'mid my wanderings meet no Anna there.

Again let us recollect that, when the Sonnet was written, the word "Faery" was fresh and radiant, and really did mean the essence of ancient romance; "charméd air" was no mere stuffed phrase, but conveyed the luxury of some incantation, and spiritual access. These notions remained unvulgarized until Keats had come to claim them in a grander manner, such as tempts the imitator. Lamb, ever afraid of excess, knew that he was to subdue his dream of wonders to the emotional and pathetic image, the fair hair, the fine beaming eye, the sense of peace, the actuality of a footstep, and forest branches, and the summer wind. If we review the devices of his poem, what are they? Nothing more than the use of plain phrase interspersed with a word or two of richer lustre or shyer growth; the repetition of plain phrase instead of some new figure, so conveying the power of his haunting.

We have a means of judging Lamb's command of poetical appropriateness at this early day. In the winter of 1794 his friend Coleridge, having abandoned his tolerant though pained College, came to town, and took up his abode

in a public-house opposite Christ's Hospital,
called the "Salutation and Cat"; where his fertile conversation is rumoured to have proved so
much for the good of the house that the landlord
offered him permanent and free entertainment.
His heart, indeed, was "yet bleeding with recent
wounds"; but neither he nor Lamb, who came to
sit through the nights with him, was to be
entirely defeated by such troubles. "Life",
wrote Lamb many years later, in an eloquent
dedication, "was fresh, and topics exhaustless,—
and you first kindled in me, if not the power, yet
the love of poetry, and beauty, and kindliness."
It was too generous a self-suppression, for Lamb
had not been previously devoid of those sympathies; but the outpouring of Coleridge's vernal
inspirations was of course a great blessing, a
gale of faith, hope and imagination. When we
examine the details of the Coleridgean magnifi-
cence acting on definite verses of Lamb's, we
find that apart from swelling themes and prologues Lamb knew best how poetry is written.
In the Sonnet which I have given, instinct had
caused Lamb to treat of the legendary as a
psychic sensation rather than as a stageable com-
modity. But Coleridge, rewriting the piece, in-
stalled the figure of Merlin waving his wizard
wand, over Lamb presumably in London streets.

Lamb showed his elder companion another Sonnet, equally serene in every quiet significance,
ending after a vision of greenwoods and Anna
thus:

> Or we might sit and tell some tender tale
> Of faithful vows repaid by cruel scorn,
> A tale of true love, or of friend forgot;
> And I would teach thee, lady, how to rail
> In gentle sort, on those who practise not
> Or love or pity, though of woman born.

That pretty fancy with its current of sad meaning
was not loud enough for Coleridge. He was for
colour, energy, and mankind; and he supplied:

> But ah! sweet scenes of fancied bliss, adieu!
> On rose-leaf beds amid your faery bowers
> I all too long have lost the dreamy hours!
> Beseems it now the sterner Muse to woo,
> If haply she her golden meed impart
> To realize the vision of the heart.

And here let me doubt whether any poet however mighty can with complete art patch up the
productions of any other poet however micro-
scopic. The idiom of each versifier appears to be
his own business, governed by considerations
not wholly shared by any other personality.

However, the first of Lamb's poems to appear
in print—in the *Morning Chronicle* of 1794—was
not only Coleridgeanized, but bore the signature

S. T. C. So far, the young clerk's acceptance of his friend's powerful superiority was his one rule in such matters. By the summer of 1796 something of independence had arisen to challenge improvement by another hand, even Coleridge's. The occasion when Lamb revealed his reflections to Coleridge was, externally, one of submission: "Poems on Various Subjects, by S. T. Coleridge, late of Jesus College, Cambridge" had just appeared, and there among the "Effusions" were specimens of Lamb's sonnets, signed C. L., but adapted to the requirements of his mentor and almost tormentor. Lamb approached the doubtful distinction in friendly candour: "In my 12th Effusion I had rather have seen what I wrote myself, tho' they bear no comparison with your exquisite lines 'On rose-leaf'd beds amid your faery bowers', &c.—I love my sonnets because they are the reflected images of my own feelings. They are dear to memory, tho' they now and then wake a sigh or a tear. 'Thinking on divers things foredone', I charge you, Col., spare my ewe lambs, and tho' a Gentleman may borrow six lines in an epic poem (I should have no objection to borrow 500 and without acknowledging) still in a Sonnet—a personal poem—I do not 'ask my friend the aiding verse'.... When my blank verse is finished,

or any long fancy poems, '*propino tibi alter-
andum, cut-up-andum, abridg-andum*', just what
you will with it—but spare my EWE LAMBS." It
is curious that about now Lamb was sending a
poem to the newly-established *Monthly Magazine*, perhaps on the invitation of his friend
George Dyer, who was closely connected with
it; and there for a year or two he was able to see
his verses in print without the attentions of a
reviser.

Other young poets now came into his circle.
In January 1795 Coleridge's friend Southey, a
youth almost as extraordinary in his passionate
outlook on his destiny, and again on what the
world should gain by it, had arrived in London
to carry Coleridge off to Bristol and the completion of their plan of a new settlement in
America. Southey visited Lamb at home—no
longer in the Temple—and, it would seem, was a
sufficient observer of Lamb's responsibilities
there not to attempt converting him to pantiso-
cracy; Lamb did not know much of Southey's
poetry until 1796, when "Joan of Arc" (with
Coleridge's share in it) "delighted, amazed"
him. "I had not presumed to expect any thing
of such excellence from Southey." At the same
time Lamb was newly aware of the promise of
William Wordsworth, as yet the northern land-

scape-painting pioneer, to whom Coleridge's attention was turning; a little later he became intimate with Charles Lloyd, who is now scarcely a name to any but the students of the early life of these Romantic poets. Lloyd had become the pupil of Coleridge, but had himself produced at Carlisle a pamphlet of poems, opening with fifteen Sonnets, pensive and confessional, and picturesque with lake scenery. Towards the end of 1796 Lloyd put forth a tall pamphlet of poems on the death of his grandmother, Priscilla Farmer, and, as he liked a manuscript piece by Lamb in memory of a Hertfordshire grandmother, he sought and obtained leave to include it.

Such circumstances taken separately would not mean much, but together they depict the growing seriousness of Lamb's poetical adventures. Moreover, his taste was being schooled in another and a more certain relation. He was already familiar with Milton and Spenser, and among the later poets, besides Bowles, had a strong understanding of Burns and Cowper especially; but on the whole he had lacked contact with the most abundant sort of poetry, that with the most daring and capable range of idea, sentiment and language. By the summer of 1796, uninstructed by his contemporaries, he had begun to move gladly in the tremendous moral and physical world of the Elizabethan dramatists. He told Coleridge of his little book of extracts, "which is full of quotations from Beaumont and Fletcher in particular"; he added also a commendation of Massinger as "treading close on their heels", themselves possessing, besides superlative simplicity and tenderness, "a greater richness of poetical fancy than any one, Shakespeare excepted". He referred to current books of criticism for companionable enthusiasm, and not finding any appealed to Coleridge to "do something to bring our elder bards into more general fame". Nearer home, he was to some extent the collaborator in a piece of Shakespearean jesting which delighted his appetite for elder bards, of passion and of mirth. His schoolfellow Jem White, who had a wonderful kindness for Sir John Falstaff, conceived the notion of turning the newly celebrated forgeries of Shakespeare to account in an innocent masquerading invention of "Original Letters &c. of Sir John Falstaff and his Friends, now first made public by a Gentleman, a Descendant of Dame Quickly". Lamb had a hand in this, having been himself the means of White's first reading the Falstaff Saga. Departing from his usual way of sonnet and blank verse, Lamb—do not stand upon niceties of external proof—thus anticipated

his prose seniority: "I am happy in presenting
the world with a series of most interesting manuscript letters, &c.—They were found by Mrs
Quickly, Landlady of the Boar Tavern in East-
cheap, in a private drawer, at the left hand corner
of a walnut-tree escritoire, the property of Sir
John Falstaff, after the good Knight's death.—
At Mrs Quickly's demise, which happened in
August 1419, they devolved, among other Out-
landish papers, such as leases, title-deeds, &c.
to her heiress at law, an elderly maiden sister;
who, unfortunately for all the world, and to my
individual eternal sorrow and regret, of all the
dishes in the culinary system, was fond of roast
pig. A curse on her Epicurean guts, that could
not be contented with plain mutton, like the rest
of her Ancestors!

"Reader, whenever, as journeying onward in
thy epistolary progress, a chasm should occur to
interrupt the chain of events, I beseech thee
blame not me, but curse the rump of roast pig.
This maiden sister, conceive with what pathos
I relate it, absolutely made use of several, no
doubt invaluable letters, to shade the jutting
protuberances of that animal from disproportion-
ate excoriation in its circuitous approaches to the
fire."

Suddenly, across Lamb's earth and sky—home

and office, poetry and wit—a thunder-stone of disaster descended. It is known to most readers of English event. Mary Lamb, her sanity collapsing under the demands of mantua-making and invalid and aged parents always with her, stabbed and killed her mother on September 22nd, 1796. Charles had had his fears already, and that morning had endeavoured, as he went to his work, to meet with the family doctor. He had not succeeded, and came home a moment after the stabbing. The blow seemed to make all that he had done elsewhere detestable. "Mention nothing of poetry", he wrote to Coleridge. "I have destroyed every vestige of past vanities of that kind." "I burned", he added later, "all my own verses, all my book of extracts from Beaumont and Fletcher and a thousand sources: I burned a little journal of my foolish passion which I had a long time kept,

> Noting ere they past away
> The little lines of yesterday."

The bonfire was a psychological necessity. The young man saw himself as obliged to clear his path for one decision, that of protecting his helpless father and sister. I have been informed that in our advanced system Mary Lamb must inevitably have been sent to Broadmoor, and some lifelong confinement of the sort was threatened in 1796; but Lamb, bending all his faculties to his purpose, gave the Home Secretary "his solemn engagement that he would take her under his care for life". That, in turn, meant the East India House for life; and it can scarcely arouse our wonder that for the moment the illusions of poetry seemed best set aside.

Presently a deeper perception of the crisis grew in him, who had from childhood been more ready than most to shape himself to and beyond his restraints and privations. He saw the future in the light of the excellence of his sister, and the happiness of his being enabled to minister to that excellence. Thus rising from his desolation, Lamb gently resumed some measure of his "past vanities". One must admit that his development as a poet had received a shock from which full recovery never came; there had been signs of his ripening into a masterly and continued accomplishment of verse, and ranking in authority of performance with Coleridge and Wordsworth. The increasing purpose had been shattered. However, within a short time, Lamb began to talk afresh of books and authors, to enquire after "Bowles's new poem on Hope"; and especially after some fugitives of his own which Coleridge had in his hands for

inclusion in the second edition of his "Poems".
Coleridge, for his part, attempted with "many
fine compliments, ingeniously decked out in the
garb of sincerity, and undoubtedly springing
from a present feeling somewhat like sincerity",
to persuade Lamb back to the exercise of verse;
he sent him, too, drafts of his own new poems,
which drew long letters of accurate critical
questioning as well as praise. If Lamb was not
to be a great poet, he was proving himself con-
scious of all that intense process of selection
which great poets must perfect; if he was not to
be moved to this kind of creation, at least he was
a sharer to an exquisite degree in its operations,
alert to its rapid incandescence, vigilant against
its superfluities or laxities. For even the highest
productions of poetry, from the "De Natura
Rerum" to the "Intimations of Immortality",
include instants below themselves, when the
spirit or the body of the writer has failed in the
task of concentrating a myriad lights and sounds
into one original symmetry. What Lamb in
1797 wrote on first reading the "Ode on the
Departing Year" makes one regret that he
could not be *perpetuated*, so that he might have
been the private secretary, so to speak, of many
a poet in many a justly illustrious poem.

With regard to his own pieces, which duly

appeared in 1797 in "Poems by S. T. Coleridge: Second Edition: to which are now added Poems by Charles Lamb, and Charles Lloyd", I have not to comment largely; for, having burned a number in despair, Lamb had not many to insert beyond those mentioned. Several additional Sonnets maintained the purity of style and pathetic sweetness of mind found in the former group, perhaps still further refined by favourite readings in Elizabethan drama—in Daniel, and Fletcher, and Jonson. Lamb had waylaid Coleridge successfully on the matter of interference. The figure of Merlin, whom Lamb condemned as liable to be taken for a conjuror of that name in Oxford Street, was given up. Lamb agreed that "not a living soul" he knew would read his verses, but still, he wished his pieces "printed verbatim his last way". A more elaborate poem, "A Vision of Repentance", was sent in time for inclusion; it is that allegory with the gravely beautiful and most musical opening,

I saw a famous fountain in my dream,
　　Where shady pathways to a valley led;
A weeping willow lay upon that stream,
　　And all around the fountain brink were spread
Wide branching trees with dark green leaf rich clad,
Forming a doubtful twilight desolate and sad.

The Vision, at that time, had a special meaning

for Lamb, being involved with his religious
thoughts on his own experiences; but Coleridge
was so hasty as to speak "slightingly" of it.
In the autumn of 1797 Coleridge (having quar-
relled with Lloyd, who was now more attracted
towards Lamb) sent to the Magazine in which
Lamb's verses found a corner occasionally "three
mock Sonnets, in ridicule of my own poems, and
Charles Lloyd's, and Charles Lamb's". These
clever, punishing parodies verged on dangerous
ground for Lamb, not so much in their ridicule
of the "affectation of unaffectedness", of man-
nerisms of word and topic, as in the burlesque
of the "fair-hair'd maid" and "lonely glade".
The next letter we have from Lamb to Coleridge
avoids the subject of poetry.

But in January 1798 Lamb threw off a poem
that has travelled farther than any he ever wrote
before or after. He himself had made fun of
attempts of Coleridge and Southey at the angli-
cising of dactylic metre. Now, by some necessity
of spirit, in uttering a sad verdict on his early
life, he played upon this recollection of Latin
and English verse, and, the rhythm springing
readily from the key-phrase of his feelings, his
poem was no mere ingenuity. It was "The Old
Familiar Faces".[1] Who will explain to us how

[1] From a note by Mrs G. A. Anderson based on

such permanent popular expressions, in verse, in prose, in music are produced; and why, while such a piece as "A Vision of Repentance" misses the mark, the same author almost immediately gives form and force to an "Old Familiar Faces"? Is it, that a certain eccentricity (as of "Alice in Wonderland" almost) is discovered in the every-day phrase and picture? for the subject itself, in Lamb's poem, in Hood's "I remember" or in a "Lead, kindly Light", or a "Crossing the Bar", is not eccentric, nor treated in any aspect which we do not all and freely possess? Something of the dream enters into the habitual. The very cadence of the household word is heard as a peculiar intimation. Objects a few doors off are seen as from beyond the grave.

I have been laughing, I have been carousing,
Drinking late, sitting late, with my bosom cronies—
All, all are gone, the old familiar faces.

I loved a love once, fairest among women,
Closed are her doors on me, I must not see her—
All, all are gone, the old familiar faces.

one by Lamb himself, it appears that this poem was written after an evening with Lloyd and White; Lloyd had played the piano, and Lamb, his feelings worked up to an uncontrollable pitch, "suddenly rushed into the Temple", and the verses followed.

I have a friend, a kinder friend has no man.
Like an ingrate, I left my friend abruptly;
Left him, to muse on the old familiar faces.

Ghost-like I paced round the haunts of my childhood.
Earth seem'd a desart I was bound to traverse,
Seeking to find the old familiar faces.

The poem, with a few others more minutely retrospective or introspective, but amounting to
little more than dignified soliloquies without
directive imagination and music, was published
in a pamphlet in 1798, and Lamb appeared once
more in a literary partnership—but not this time
with his schoolfellow. "Blank Verse, by Charles
Lloyd and Charles Lamb", represented an inevitable secession. There was at least one notice
of it, which may be consoling to our young poets
who envy Keats his lengthy allowances of abuse,
for it shows the superior steel of brevity; after
insulting Lloyd, the *Monthly Review* observed
that "Mr Lamb, the joint author of this little
volume, seems to be very properly associated
with his plaintive companion".

Yet "Blank Verse" revealed to Lamb that he
was in a manner a public character. In July 1798
the poets of the *Anti-Jacobin*, who had several
times made joyful holiday over the works of the
friends of Liberty, the new poets, began to in-

clude Lamb in their target—not improbably because in his evening leisure he was seen now
and then in the company of reformists. A grand
spectacle in verse was worked up, called "The
New Morality", in which an absurd Benedicite
was produced for the good of a French atheist
called Lepaux.

> And ye five other wandering Bards, that move
> In sweet accord of harmony and love,
> C—dge and S—th—y, L—d, and L—be and Co.
> Tune all your mystic harps to praise Lepaux!

Soon afterwards there appeared one of Gillray's
uproarious caricatures, illustrating the "New
Morality". At one end of the room on a platform that gargantuan artist enthroned Justice,
Philanthropy, Sensibility (the last looking very
much like Mr Low's views of Mr Maxton); a
host of monsters big and little were drawn
offering a mad hymn to these three. Two don-
keys—Coleridge was never let off for his "Lines
to a Young Ass"—were intended for Coleridge
and Southey, one offering a paper of "Dacty-
lics", the other of "Saphics"; squatted on the
floor behind them, two inflated creatures were
shown croaking with great satisfaction to a paper
they held up, inscribed "BLANK VERSE by Toad
& Frog". Do not let us lay this to our souls as

a token that our society has progressed far from
such maltreatment of our poets. It has still other
ways of making monsters of them.

Diverging from verse again, Lamb in 1798
published a curious prose-poem, an idyllic tragedy, called "Rosamund Gray". It was an
experiment, developed from the style of Henry
Mackenzie the novelist of sensibility; the silences
many, the sentences brief, the transitions sudden. The description of the heroine may stand
for the effect which Lamb had in his aspiration:
"Her face had the sweetest expression in it—a
gentleness—a modesty—a timidity—a certain
charm—a grace without a name". That grace is
partially gained, enough to have taken Shelley;
the "miniature romance" has something of the
sunshine and blossom, the intruding demon and
storm of German ballad. Lamb next endeavoured
the composition of a drama "of laughter and
tears, prose and verse; and, in some places,
rhyme". He called it at first "Pride's Cure",
and later "John Woodvil"—under which title it
appeared in a volume in 1802; but it occupied
him until the close of 1800. This, too, was an
experiment. Lamb had found the style of the
plainer plays of his Elizabethans concurrent with,
and stimulating to, his own natural old-fashioned
expression; and he ventured to show what he

could do independent of the Sheridanesque cleverness around him. In the result, "John Woodvil" had not the robustness of verse, character or conversation to be more than a pleasant interlude, of which the chief merit is a spirit of country life, and that found essentially in one happy passage—Elia among the nature-poets! At least, the passage was first printed in a magazine called *Recreations in Agriculture.*

Margaret. What sports do you use in the forest?
Simon. Not many; some few, as thus:

> To see the sun to bed, and to arise,
> Like some hot amourist with glowing eyes,
> Bursting the lazy bands of sleep that bound him,
> With all his fires and travelling glories round
>   him.
> Sometimes the moon on soft night clouds to rest,
> Like beauty nestling in a young man's breast,
> And all the winking stars, her handmaids, keep
> Admiring silence, while those lovers sleep.
> Sometimes outstretcht, in very idleness,
> Nought doing, saying little, thinking less,
> To view the leaves, thin dancers upon air,
> Go eddying round; and small birds, how they
>   fare
> When mother Autumn fills their beaks with corn,
> Filch'd from the careless Amalthea's horn;
> And how the woods berries and worms provide,
> Without their pains, when earth has nought beside
> To answer their small wants.

To view the graceful deer come tripping by,
Then stop, and gaze, then turn, they know not
why,
Like bashful younkers in society.
To mark the structure of a plant or tree,
And all fair things of earth, how fair they be,
Margaret (*smiling*). And, afterwards them paint in
simile.

At this point, Lamb left the eighteenth century
and his poethood behind him. In later years, he
wrote many verses, some of which must be
admitted even to my epitome of a various mind
and authorship; but they were desultory, and
nothing was farther from his purpose than to
build up a mansion of theory and practice of
poetry as his contemporaries Coleridge, Wordsworth, Southey were doing. Once, as I have
suggested, he had seemed to be in prospect of
such an evolution of spirit and art. But already
he had fallen out of the high calling, except as an
intimate visitor. He had, personally, made up a
quarrel with Coleridge, incidental to a reported
remark of that not always intelligent great man
on Lamb's defects of intelligence. Lamb to
Coleridge on that occasion was as unanswerable
as any problem ever set before the philosopher.
Nevertheless, when in November 1798 the new
alliance of Wordsworth and Coleridge sent out

that statement of true poetry called the "Lyrical
Ballads", of which the proposals still stimulate
and the performance still challenges our poetry,
Lamb was not missing. He reproved Southey
heartily for failing to give the "Ancient Mariner"
its rank. He almost "degenerated into abuse"
as he insisted on "fifty passages as miraculous
as the miracles they celebrate"; it was a more
energizing poem even than "Tintern Abbey",
"which is yet one of the finest written". Lamb's
first letter of the nineteenth century, to Wordsworth, presents his close considerations on the
second volume of the "Lyrical Ballads", un-
selfish and vital, because not all-swallowing,
appreciation; but at the end is a postscript in
which one may catch not only a complaint against
Wordsworth's egotism, but the voice of a
secretly disappointed poet—"Thank you for
Liking my Play!!"

CHAPTER III

CHARLES AND MARY

"In describing her brother", wrote a friend of
Mary Lamb, "we describe her. Her heart and
her intellect have been through life the counter-
part of his own. The two have lived as one, in
double singleness together. She has been, indeed, the supplement and completion of his
existence." These words, which make one think
of the "Phoenix and Turtle" and a solution
hardly intended by Shakespeare, apply to the
whole of Lamb's life; but there was a period
during which Charles and Mary were co-
operative as authors especially, and to that decade—from 1801 to 1811—my sketch now comes.
In the year 1799 John Lamb the elder had died,
and Mary's life became solely interwoven
(friendships apart) with that of her younger
brother. At the turn of the century the two
moved to Mitre Court Buildings, within the
Temple, and there they remained for most of
the period I am about to notice. "I can see the

white sails glide by the bottom of the King's
Bench walks", Lamb boasted to Manning, "as I
lie in my bed." This Manning demands our
consideration even at the expense of vignettes
of the lamented white sails, and blue hills of
Surrey.

He was a mathematical tutor at Cambridge,
and assisted Lamb with the first proposition of
Euclid—but Lamb's regard for him did not find
its abiding reason in that fact. He was a man of
general abilities, but one cannot find him out in
the shades of the great. He was, it seems, in part
Lamb's creation, like "Elia"; Lamb brought
out in Manning the quality which he scarcely
suspected not to be there for everybody to en-
joy, and from Manning, in some way that
Manning's brisk letters to him do not desig-
nate, Lamb drew impulses for his finest and
artfullest humour. The first meeting of these
friends was at the close of 1799, in Cambridge.
Immediately, as Lear was fascinated by Edgar
in disguise, Lamb was magnetized by Manning,
and a series of long and merry letters, each a
literary possession, began. To him, early in
1801, went a glorious report on the conse-
quences of Lamb's having made some reser-
vations in his thanks for the new "Lyrical Ballads". "All the North of England are in a

turmoil. Cumberland and Westmoreland have already declared a state of war." Wordsworth, though troubled with "an almost insurmountable aversion to letter-writing", had not missed a post to retort—in "four sweating pages"— "that he was sorry his 2d vol. had not given me more pleasure (Devil a hint did I give that it had *not pleased me*), and 'was compelled to wish that my range of sensibility was more extended, being obliged to believe that I should receive large influxes of happiness and happy thoughts' —(I suppose from the L. B.)—With a deal of stuff about a certain Union of Tenderness and Imagination, which in the sense he used Imagination was not the characteristic of Shakspeare, but which Milton possessed in a degree far exceeding other Poets: which Union, as the highest species of Poetry, and chiefly deserving that name, 'He was most proud to aspire to'; then illustrating the said Union by two quotations from his own 2d vol. (which I had been so unfortunate as to miss)....This was not to be *all* my castigation. Coleridge, who had not written to me some months before, starts up from his bed of sickness to reprove me for my hardy presumption: four long pages equally sweaty and more tedious, came from him; assuring me that, when the works of a man of true genius such as W. undoubtedly was, do not please me at first sight, I should suspect the fault to lie 'in me and not in them', etc. etc. etc. etc. etc."

I borrow these excerpts not solely for the jokes but as an instance of Lamb's ironic vigour when he had a man to talk with. Equally, the conviction that Manning understood all produced in Lamb his most triumphant humanities. "I must confess that I am not romance-bit about *Nature*....Streets, streets, streets, markets, theatres, churches, Covent Gardens, shops sparkling with pretty faces of industrious milliners, neat sempstresses, ladies cheapening, gentlemen behind counters lying, authors in the street with spectacles, George Dyers (you may know them by their gait), lamps lit at night, pastry-cooks' and silver-smiths' shops, beautiful Quakers of Pentonville, noise of coaches, drowsy cry of mechanic watchman at night, with bucks reeling home drunk; if you happen to wake at midnight, cries of Fire and Stop thief; inns of court, with their learned air, and halls, and butteries, just like Cambridge colleges; old book-stalls, Jeremy Taylors, Burtons on Melancholy and Religio Medicis on every stall. These are thy pleasures, O London with-the-many-sins." Then, too, Manning called into action Lamb's full power of

whimsical fabrication; as when he sent Lamb a
present of brawn, bought of one Hopkins, which
summoned up a most plausible history, beginning thus: "Dear Manning,—I have been very
unwell since I saw you. A sad depression of
spirits, a most unaccountable nervousness; from
which I have been partially relieved by an odd
accident. You knew Dick Hopkins, the swearing
scullion of Caius? This fellow, by industry and
agility, has thrust himself into the important
situation (no sinecures, believe me) of cook to
Trinity Hall and Caius College: and the generous
creature has contrived with the greatest delicacy imaginable, to send me a present of Cambridge brawn. What makes it the more extraordinary is, that the man never saw me in his
life that I know of. I suppose he has *heard* of
me....We have not many such men in any rank
of life as Mr R. Hopkins". And yet all this and
more of the sort is only the garnish of a fantasy
on the "reserved collegiate worth of brawn",
in comparisons with the pictures of the "choice
old Italian masters", Wordsworth's poetry, and
other stately subjects.

But Manning departed into China in 1806,
and Lamb was still gathering other friends about
him. A young man still, he had long learned
what is often to the last a baffling lesson, the

supreme pleasure of friendship in many degrees or chords. Early in 1800 he had, after an unpromising start, collected that embarrassing ambiguous philosopher William Godwin. How far these two matured their mutual esteem, is hard to judge; did anyone ever arrive at affection for the hard-reasoned Godwin? It is odd that one or two of Lamb's few curt notes are addressed to him, one,[1] really angry, refusing for the last time to let him print a fragmentary criticism on Chaucer (which, accordingly, has vanished utterly). Yet Godwin is important in the story of Charles and Mary Lamb, not because he had supplied the world and them with a provisional manual of perfectibility, but as a fountain of wonder, amusement and even employment. The wonder lay in Godwin's—the Professor's—cool

[1] "My dear sir, I assure you positively that what I had begun to write about Chaucer was so inconsiderable that you could make no possible use of it. I have it not, and if I could recover it I should be extremely hurt to be obliged to show it you. I beg you to let the matter now rest, and unless you wish to tease and vex me, that you will not mention it again. I hoped that I had said enough before. Yours truly, C. Lamb." (From Miss I. A. Taylor's article "On Autographs", in *Longman's Magazine*, June 1891.)

perspective of a mind, by means of which all sub-
lunary agitation and enigma became, or seemed
to become, controlled and explicit. The amusement was partly derived from that same sublimity where it trod the waters of the ridiculous.
Let us hear Mary Lamb on one of Godwin's re-
forms: "He took his usual walk one evening, a
fortnight since, to the end of Hatton Garden and
back again. During that walk, a thought came
into his mind, which he instantly set down and
improved upon, till he brought it, in seven or
eight days, into the compass of a reasonable
sized pamphlet. To propose a subscription to
all well disposed people, to be expended in the
care of a cheap monument for the former and the
future great dead men,—the monument to be a
white cross, with a wooden slab at the end,
telling their names and qualifications. This
wooden slab and white cross to be perpetuated
to the end of time. To survive the fall of empires
and the destruction of cities by means of a map,
which was, in case of an insurrection among the
people, or any other cause by which a city or
country may be destroyed, to be carefully preserved; and then, when things got again into
their usual order, the white-cross-wooden-slab-
makers were to go to work again, and set them
in their former places. This, as nearly as I can

tell you, is the sum and substance of it, but it is written remarkably well, in his very best manner".

The employment was of a more immediate and more effective description, and recalls me to the chief topic of this chapter—Charles and Mary. But for Godwin, the united names might not have signified what they do and have done in a difficult and delightful province of literature. By his advice and publishing activity, the brother and sister were enabled to take their place among the few enduring creators of books for children —and that has been matter for wonderment, that the bachelor and the old maid in their childlessness should have so excelled a host of authors and authoresses better placed for a comprehension of the task they undertook. Charles appeared first in this enterprise; in 1805 Godwin set up in business as a bookseller and one of his earliest ideas was "The King and Queen of Hearts" with drawings by young William Mulready, the text in rhyme by Lamb. It calls for no other remark at the moment. Next, the suggestion was made that the Lambs should make tales for children out of twenty of Shakespeare's plays. Something like this plan had been tried by a French writer; subsequently we meet with variations on it often enough—Tales from

Chaucer, Spenser, Virgil and so on, which still
do not vie with the "Tales from Shakespear"
in initial problems and in universal acceptance.
By June 1806 the brother and sister had made
great progress, "writing on one table", so
Mary Lamb described their work, "(but not on
one cushion sitting) like Hermia and Helena in
the Midsummer Night's Dream; or rather, like
an old literary Darby and Joan: I taking snuff,
and he groaning all the while, and saying he can
make nothing of it, which he always says till he
has finished, and then he finds out he has made
something of it".

Charles provided paraphrases of six of the
Tragedies. The first decision that he and his
sister took was to avoid the Shakespearean way
of bringing in the general situation and leading
personages by means of subsidiary people and
talk, and to set before his juvenile audience at
once the giants of the history. The curtain rose,
and at once: "Lear, King of Britain, had three
daughters; Gonerill, wife to the duke of Albany;
Regan, wife to the duke of Cornwall; and Cordelia, a young maid, for whose love the king of
France and duke of Burgundy were joint suitors,
and were at this time making stay for that purpose in the court of Lear". Then, dialogue was
largely reduced, but often the shrewd and mo-

mentous expression was incorporated in the narrative; "Shakespear's words are used whenever
it seemed possible to bring them in". Incidentally Lamb sometimes preserved a word of which
the meaning is not quite fixed, and gave with it
his explanation. Thus, in allusion to that phrase
"the dukes of waterish Burgundy", he remarked,
"he called the duke of Burgundy in contempt
a waterish duke, because his love for this young
maid had in a moment run all away like water".
Or more concisely: Hamlet's father, he said, was
poisoned not with hebenon, but henbane. Sometimes he pointed out a nicety: adding a parenthe-
tical "as she prettily expressed it" to Cordelia's
saying that her enemy's dog, though it had bit
her, should have stayed by her fire on such a
night. It was thought by the writers that
Charles's best Tale was "Othello".

Mary, with her fourteen Comedies, had the
more awkward task, where so much of the
original beauty and interest dwelt in the minute
sequence of the dialogue, and the plots were so
much more intricate. She too handled the problem of substituting narrative for drama with
boldness. "The Merchant of Venice" was made
to open not with Antonio's little group of friends
in every-day talk, but with this: "Shylock, the
Jew, lived at Venice: he was an usurer, who had

amassed an immense fortune by lending money
at great interest to Christian merchants". In
her version of this play, Mary abandoned the
casket scenes—one wonders why; perhaps she
found them forced. In "Much Ado About
Nothing", she omitted Dogberry, presumably
because children were hardly skilled enough in
hard words to catch the point of his "comprehending two auspicious persons" or "condemned
into everlasting redemption"; but the same
Tale yields a good instance of her willingness to
face difficulties with insight. When Hero, ac-
cused in the church, falls in a swoon, Claudio
and his friends depart in an abrupt way, not easy
to accept; Mary Lamb records it exactly and
comments "So hard-hearted had their anger
made them". For the opening of "A Midsummer Night's Dream", she makes it the law
of Athens, by which daughters refusing to marry
the men chosen by their fathers should be put to
death; she adds agreeably that it is not customary
with fathers to have their daughters executed
"even though they do happen to prove a little
refractory"; and then with finely pointed verisimilitude she proceeds, "There was one instance,
however, of an old man...who actually did come
before Theseus...".

Both for style and matter the "Tales from

Shakespear" were regarded from the first edition (January 1807) as a classic. Of course, not all critics concurred. "We should have been happy", said one, "had something like morals been deduced from such incidents as afford them; and indeed we have long since determined that no book intended for youth is deserving of praise which does not either explicitly or implicitly promote virtue, general or particular." Morals were then, to many, a kind of directions on every bottle. It is impossible to count the number of later editions. Mary's name did not appear on the title-page of the first six. In 1831 the eleventh edition contained William Harvey's popular illustrations. Sir John Gilbert's did not arrive until 1866, Arthur Rackham's until 1899, Heath Robinson's until 1902. There were three new illustrated editions in 1923. These are the results of Godwin's commencing bookseller and enlisting Charles and Mary Lamb in his cause. Lamb grumbled a little when he saw the book: the plates were not his choice, and "in the first place" Godwin had "cheated me by putting a name to [the Tales] which I did not mean, but do not repent". Before the first edition was out, Mary had "begun a new work", which occupied her a year, and gave her a reputation among those best qualified to give it under the name of

Mrs Leicester. It was a collection of tales, or
sketches from nature rather, under the title
"Mrs Leicester's School: or the History of
Several Young Ladies Related by Themselves";
ten tales, of which Charles Lamb wrote three.
It was said of this book—how justly I do not
decide, for to my mind there were many excellent
women (I do not count Mrs Markham) then
writing for children: "She is the only writer for
children who seems to have a fitting respect for
those whom she addresses. She does not feel
for infancy merely as a season of ignorance and
want. She knows that it is also the time of
reverence and wonder—of confiding love and
boundless hope—of 'splendour in the grass, of
glory in the flower'". And, indeed, both her
tales and her brother's seem to me extra-
ordinarily sensitive in their impression of the
world in which children move, and those things
which to a child seem oddly important and, even
if inanimate, possess life and influence. How
those early chimaeras, or primitive pieties, desert
most grown-up memories! "Mrs Leicester's"
book was issued at the end of 1808; by 1825 the
ninth edition was called for; and in modern re-
prints it still justifies Coleridge's belief that it
was a permanent enrichment of our literature,—
but how long shall we or our children desire and

respond to such quiet, sweet, sequestered perfections?

I must here illustrate the quaint unexpected critical hobgoblins which awaited Mrs Leicester. "We might", said a fairly unhostile reviewer, "have admitted this production to a place among those intended to diversify the attention of youth, had we not detected in it a too great importance attached to theatrical enjoyments."

Before that book was ready, Godwin published Lamb's own variation on the idea of "Tales from Shakespear"—namely, his "Adventures of Ulysses", which he said with a grin was "intended to be an introduction to the reading of Telemachus", that morality of Fénélon's. Over this little book, founded on Chapman's translation of the "Odyssey", Lamb had a skirmish with Godwin, who, superior as his soul was to the littleness of society, yet was for being quite punctilious, and requested for the benefit of "a squeamish age" the omission of several lively passages. Only one bowdlerism would Lamb yield. His "Adventures" he arranged not in the order of our Homer, but consecutively from Troy to Ithaca: "in this", says Dr E. A. Gardner in his edition of the book published here in 1921, "Lamb is very likely going back to the original form of the poem"—

which would have filled Lamb with nonsensical self-approval. The writing in this book is simple and noble, in close understanding of Chapman's achievement; and Dr Gardner shows Lamb following Chapman's occasional errors. But then, Chapman's Homer was one of the books which Lamb in his wild fancies would give a kiss to— "my midnight darlings! my folios".

The prodigious money value of certain issues of the Lambs' books for children has produced a few attributions—as, of "Felissa, a Kitten of Sentiment", and the "Book of Ranks"—which are not warranted; it may be that Charles and Mary did indeed authorize a few more of these fragile recreations as yet unidentified. A well-known one, now to be mentioned, vanished for half a century. "Poetry for Children" appeared from Godwin's Juvenile Library in 1809, having been written by the authors that spring. "Our poems", wrote Lamb to Coleridge, rejoicing to have finished a task, "are but humble, but they have no name. You must read them, remembering they were task-work; and perhaps you will admire the number of subjects, all of children, picked out by an old Bachelor and an old Maid. Many parents would not have found so many." The poems had as rivals the similar collections of Jane and Ann Taylor, which far outran them

in public reward. Yet there were judges who
found "something of a higher cast" in the poetry
of "Mrs Leicester"—"a deep humanity, which
cannot fail to nurture and to mellow the opening heart, to render its seriousness sweeter, and
its joy deeper and more lasting". Many of the
pieces indeed are genuinely poems, serious or
humorous. The writers have been in earnest,
and their consciousness of an audience has only
restricted them in choice of theme and vocabulary; they do not otherwise distrust or cajole the
child's wits. Witness this:

Horatio, of ideal courage vain,
Was flourishing in air his father's cane,
And as the fumes of valour swell'd his pate,
Now thought himself *this* Hero, and now *that*:
"And now", he cried, "I will Achilles be;
My sword I brandish; see, the Trojans flee.
Now I'll be Hector, when his angry blade
A lane through heaps of slaughter'd Grecians
    made!
And now by deeds still braver I'll evince
I am no less than Edward the Black Prince.—
Give way, ye coward French:—" as thus he spoke,
And aim'd in fancy a sufficient stroke
To fix the fate of Cressy or Poictiers
(The muse relates the Hero's fate with tears)
He struck his milk-white hand against a nail,
Sees his own blood, and feels his courage fail.

Ah! where is now that boasted valour flown,
That in the tented field so late was shown!
Achilles weeps, Great Hector hangs his head,
And the Black Prince goes whimpering to bed.

The poets did not think it unfitting for the
imagination of children to be moved by natural
sadness, even by tragic wonder. This is Charles
Lamb's:

Smiling river, smiling river,
  On thy bosom sun-beams play;
Though they're fleeting, and retreating,
  Thou hast more deceit than they.

In thy channel, in thy channel,
  Choak'd with ooze and grav'lly stones,
Deep immersed, and unhearsed,
  Lies young Edward's corse: his bones

Ever whitening, ever whitening,
  As thy waves against them dash;
What thy torrent, in the current,
  Swallow'd, now it helps to wash.

As if senseless, as if senseless
  Things had feeling in this case;
What so blindly, and unkindly,
  It destroy'd, it now does grace.

Apart from a pamphlet called "Prince Dorus",
the Lambs appear to have concluded their con-
tributions to children's literature with these
Poems; and perhaps I have hovered too long

over their little series of books, celebrated as they are. Yet I have done so as aware of a great common-sense, and at the same time a romantic faith towards the education of children, in Charles and Mary Lamb, themselves imperfectly schooled yet how admirably educated—a collateral moderation and liberty, guidance and unconcern, which I feel to be valuable, and wish it might be prevalent now. From their tradition should spring care, reasonable hope, decent pride; but Charles Lamb has explained better at the end of the preface to the "Tales from Shakespear": "What these Tales have been to you in childhood, that and much more it is my wish that the true Plays of Shakespear may prove to you in older years—enrichers of the fancy, strengtheners of virtue, a withdrawing from all selfish and mercenary thoughts, a lesson of all sweet and honourable thoughts and actions, to teach you courtesy, benignity, generosity, humanity". An old-fashioned prescription.

It was well that Lamb should meet with some good fortune in one part of his authorship, in his thirties, for he suffered enough disappointments otherwise. No manager would take "John Woodvil" for the stage, and the author, printing it at his own cost, not only lost money but was assailed with scornful reviews. The money he

could not afford to drop. His India House income
was only £160 a year so late as 1809. He
attempted to obtain regular engagements as a
journalist. The *Morning Chronicle*, for example,
was a flourishing newspaper. Most of his articles
there were rejected, and turning to the *Morning
Post* he was permitted to do a little, and that
little "very irksome, and rendered ten times
more so from a sense of my employer not being
fully satisfied". He hit on a congenial way of
expressing his whims and wisdom, and projected
a series of papers under the general head "The
Londoner"; the first, as printed in the *Morning
Post*, made Manning tell him he should write a
volume of essays in the style. But Lamb was ill
at ease in the *Morning Post*, and his resignation
was received very willingly by the editor. After
some time he again formed the hope—recurrent
through his life—that he should produce a something for the theatre. The trouble was to make
time, and find peace, for the work. In February
1806 he reported: "Have taken a room at *3s.* a
week, to be in between *5* and *8* at night, to
avoid my *nocturnal* alias *knock-eternal* visitors.
The first-fruits of my retirement has been a farce
which goes to a manager to-morrow. *Wish my
ticket luck*". The farce thus committed to the
lottery-wheel was to be the most famous failure

in our theatrical history, yet in itself a slight
affair.

"Sir", wrote the Manager of Drury Lane
theatre that June, "Your Piece of Mr H——
I am desired to say is accepted by the Proprietors, and, if agreeable to you, will be brought
forward when the proper opportunity serves."
Lamb was, like Bottom, temporarily translated.
He even wrote to Wordsworth to share the
good news. The rehearsals were secret, for the
point of Mr H—— was that the full name of that
gentleman should not come out prematurely.
Some public excitement was worked up. Elliston
was playing the mysterious hero's part. On
Dec. 10, 1806, the house was crowded; the
author, with two friends not yet mentioned,
Hazlitt and Crabb Robinson, sat in the front
row of the pit. The Prologue was recited by
Elliston, there were shouts of "encore", and
Lamb in the manner of Charlie Chaplin shouted
"encore". After these brilliant couplets (which
were appreciated *then*), there was a diminishing
applause, and by the end of the first Act "the
friends of the author began to fear". Too
reasonably; not long after the resumption Mr
H.'s secret was revealed, the name he had been
so uncomfortably concealing proved to be Hogsflesh (one of Lamb's schoolfellows was named

Hogsflesh), and impatience broke into hisses (to which Lamb added his own) before the concluding alteration of Mr H.'s surname by royal licence to Bacon. Even so, it was Elliston's belief that the farce might be put on again, but Lamb almost jubilantly requested that it should be left alone, in its glory of one night only.

In a letter making the best of "the failure of our little farce", Mary Lamb gave notice of still another literary project of her brother's, which was also fated to be disappointing in its immediate reception, but which Lamb always regarded as a work to be proud of. "My brother", wrote Mary, "sometimes threatens to pass his holidays in town hunting over old plays at the Museum to extract passages for a work (a collection of poetry) Mr Wordsworth intends to publish." On a previous occasion we saw Lamb appealing to Coleridge for a re-creation of older English poetry; now, with the same modesty, he was hoping that Wordsworth would stand forth in this action on behalf of true taste and the genius of rich but forgotten imaginations. Neither Coleridge nor Wordsworth gave the answer that he looked for, and he was constrained (and fortunately) to advance himself as the champion of his old poets. In February 1808 he could place before Manning at Canton the

articles of his new book. "[It is] done for
Longman, and is 'Specimens of English Dramatic Poets contemporary with Shakespear'.
Specimens are becoming fashionable. We have—
'Specimens of Ancient English Poets', 'Specimens of Modern English Poets', 'Specimens of
Ancient English Prose-Writers', without end.
They used to be called 'Beauties'. You have
seen 'Beauties of Shakespear'? so have many
people that never saw any beauties in Shakespear. Longman is to print it, and be at all the
expense and risk; and I am to share the profits
after all deductions; *i.e.* a year or two hence I
must pocket what they please to tell me is due
to me. But the book is such as I am glad there
should be. It is done out of old plays at the
Museum and out of Dodsley's collection, &c.
It is to have notes. So I go creeping on since
I was lamed with that cursed fall from off the
top of Drury-Lane Theatre into the pit, something more than a year ago. However, I have
been free of the house ever since, and the house
was pretty free with me upon that occasion.
Damn 'em, how they hissed!"

Lamb's "Specimens" were published in 1808,
a volume of almost 500 pages. Let me glance
at the book in relation to the library of Elizabethan poetry. Lamb himself, in his Preface,

informs us very fairly of what was commonly
accessible when he set to work. The eighteenth
century had done something for the ordinary
reader in this subject, apart from its splendid
editions of Shakespeare. Several scholars had
superintended sets of Beaumont and Fletcher;
more than one had provided Ben Jonson afresh;
and there were certain considerable collections
of various composition. So far back as 1744
Robert Dodsley had published "A Select Collection of Old Plays" (twelve volumes) which
was re-edited by Isaac Reed in 1780 (though
Reed's edition was partly destroyed by fire
later). In 1773 Thomas Hawkins had brought
out at Oxford his three volumes of "The Origin
of the English Drama illustrated by Specimens
from our earliest writers". I am far from suggesting that these few titles comprise all that
had been done prior to 1808; the eighteenth
century was far too zealous in pursuit of curious
antiquities not to have produced much more,
and even as I write I am reminded of such a work
as Beloe's "Anecdotes of Literature and Scarce
Books", which began to appear in 1806. Beloe,
as an assistant librarian at the British Museum,
must have been making his notes at the same
time as Lamb. Yet, all said and done, the
character of these worthy eighteenth-century dis-

coverers was—Doctor Syntax. The antiquary's
spectacles and snuff-box lay on the pages they
so gravely reprinted. Lamb came with a different
and a profounder reverence. He read not relics
but realities, not costume and custom but glory,
life and spirit. I postpone some part of my too
dry inspection, but may borrow Mr Lucas's
words on the "Specimens": "It is not a text-
book. It is an inspired but strictly unofficial
invitation, as informal and privileged as a
familiar letter, to visit a great tract of beautiful
and wonderful country".

Had Lamb been a seer of things to come, he
might have accepted smilingly the failure of the
first edition of his "Specimens" to bring in even
a pittance in return for his holiday toils, which
must have been intense. For every one of his
500 pages, there had been ten or twenty to read,
mark, learn, and digest; as in all that he did,
speaking or writing, his chosen final expression,
however aerial it pretended to be, was drawn
from depths of painful observation and reconsideration. Lamb would have been the man to
understand, for example, the substructure and
the surface of Japanese poems of a few syllables,
or petals. To return, his reward for his labours
was next to nothing; the ostensible "Second
Edition" was nothing but the unsold sheets,

equipped with a new title-page. And the reviewers? Some[1] liked his book; some merely
sneered, and what made their sneering worse
was their literary ignorance, with nobody to
check it. The worst incident in the early history
of Lamb's almost sacred offering to British poetry
and feeling came a year or two later, when
Scott's friend Weber had produced an edition of
Ford and the *Quarterly Review* attended to it.
"We have", observed the *Quarterly*, "a more
serious charge to bring against the editor than
the omission of points, or the misapprehension
of words. He has polluted his pages with the
blasphemies of a poor maniac, who, it seems,
once published some detached scenes of the
'Broken Heart'. For this unfortunate creature,
every feeling mind will find an apology in his
calamitous situation; but for Mr Weber, we
know not where the warmest of his friends will
find palliation or excuse." In case it were
thought that this critic really referred to madness in Lamb's family, his letter is extant declaring that he knew nothing at all of that. He
merely wished to destroy the angel. Neverthe-

[1] It is agreeable to find the furious young J. G.
Lockhart of *Blackwood's* approving of the "Specimens" a little later; but I do not know that he
published his approval.

less, Lamb seems to have had some conviction
that what he had attempted was not to be destroyed by such north-easters. Before long,
beyond the circle of his intimates, evidence that
he did not err began to appear. Editing George
Chapman, the accurate S. W. Singer would describe Lamb's book as "a selection in which are
displayed the utmost judgment and taste. The
critical notices are extremely valuable, and above
any praise of mine". Later in the century would
come Dyce, later again A. H. Bullen, in whom
the spirit of the old antiquaries was rectified by
Lamb's lesson in the essentials of poetry, with
the result that the Elizabethan dramatists were
at length fully revealed. Nor is the influence of
Lamb's anthology and appreciative passion extinct, though reprints grow rarer; without his
light, I can hardly think we should have proceeded from Dyce and Bullen to such skilful
editors and vivid annotators as Mr Bonamy
Dobree and Mr F. L. Lucas.

I cannot keep out an instance of the sort of
opposition which, apart from the virulence of
the old *Quarterly*, Lamb's mind, following the
gleam of the "Specimens", has encountered in
the hundred years. Fifty years after he made
that fine present to the spirit of man, one of his
admirers, and a valuable student of literature,

complained: "It is much to be regretted that a collection disfigured by so many indecencies ever won its way into public favour; and no man confers a benefit upon society by 'renewing a taste for the great contemporaries of Shakespeare' so long as he renews at the same time a taste for their abominable obscenities".

Out of a great many friends who through this period of partial disappointment and uncertain direction assembled at Lamb's, one or two require a notice before we pass further. Some, the Burneys, the musical critic Ayrton, the philosophic Basil Montagu, the unhappy George Burnett, are for a fuller and a fire-side history; though the last two, as editors of specimens of the old prose writers whom Lamb delighted in, illustrate the literary life of Lamb. Two others, whom we caught sight of at the unique performance of "Mr H——", are of a stronger persistency. William Hazlitt, the glad extremes of whose opinion and manner now win him disciples at the expense of his chief inspirer Lamb, entered Lamb's world about the year 1804. The two men were much of the same age, and were attracted alike by books, pictures, and truths rescued from the den of error. Hazlitt was masterly in one study which Lamb did not warmly share,—philosophical system; so much so, that later on Keats would decide to approach him for instruction in that. But so far, the philosophic critic was not dominant; Hazlitt was part of his time a portrait painter, part even—according to Lamb—a writer of verses and "pretty things in prose". His conversation quickly stimulated Lamb in much the same way as Manning's, not, I think, supplying Lamb with ideas he had not already but causing him to exert and enlarge his utterances, confident because of Hazlitt. "The proudest of my life", wrote Elia in 1823, defining the years in which Hazlitt's friendship had been securely his; and in 1830 Lamb was one of the few who watched over Hazlitt's deathbed, all the temporary irritable disparagements with which Hazlitt had mingled his appreciations having done no damage to an exemplary understanding.

Henry Crabb Robinson was indebted to Mrs Clarkson, the wife of Thomas Clarkson the reformer and emancipator, for his first meetings with Wordsworth and with Lamb; but it is almost equally fair to say that Wordsworth and Lamb were indebted on this score. Robinson published nothing that matters now, but he left that enormous accumulation of diaries, notebooks, and correspondence from which it is seen that he was an essential collaborator in the life-work of a host of eminent friends. On his old house at Bury St Edmunds the commemorative tablet gives him the none too lustrous appellation, *Diarist*; now, no one can deny his claim to wisdom in resolving to record copiously the private talk and characteristics of his men of genius, but the term falls short of his value. Crabb Robinson was born, like Lamb, in 1775; through Hazlitt, he became aware of the "Lyrical Ballads and the poems generally of Words- worth, Coleridge, Lamb and Southey" by the end of the century. He began the nineteenth century by staying several years in Germany, acquiring all that he could of the spirit of the poets and philosophers, and by his devotedness playing a part in their campaign. Returning to England rich in his especial experiences, he soon found means to become acquainted with Charles and Mary Lamb. Further journeys abroad in- terrupted the acquaintance, but he contrived, as we saw, to be with Lamb at his other "first play"; moreover, he attended and recommended Coleridge's lectures in 1808. Early in 1810 he expressed an interest which he had already shown in William Blake's poetry and paintings by sending a memoir of him to a new German magazine. He had already gained the regard and stirred the intellect of Wordsworth in a

"battle arranged nicely by Charles Lamb's
fireside". He now listened with admiration to
the monologues of Coleridge. In short, by the
end of 1810, Crabb Robinson had established
himself among those English personalities who
were reanimating thought and word as a necessary counsellor, liaison officer, or touchstone of
normality; one, as Lamb called him, "unwearied
in the offices of a friend". In him, we see a type
without which even the liveliest originators
might grow purposeless, a walking canon of
criticism without whom the best imagination
might fall into eccentricity, and a trustee of
common affairs which in his absence must have
frequently impeded or suppressed moments of
vision. Camden was praised as the "nourrice
of antiquity"; Crabb Robinson should be
honoured as the nourrice of futurity.

CHAPTER IV

THE NEW CRITICISM

It was hardly Lamb's way to whip one topic on the back of another, and in literary judgments he seldom drew a contrast between the improved present and the foolish past. From the eighteenth-century library he, like Wordsworth, drew much of his own pleasure and attainment. A minute perusal of his quotations and echoes, and even of his explicit allusions to chapter and verse, will attest that he did not forget, under the spell of Webster, and Sir Thomas Browne, and Wither, and Burton, what had been done by Pope, and Prior, and Collins, and Shenstone—by Swift, Defoe, and Smollett. He was the last man to indulge a hostility of mind towards their age, by way of heightening a rapture elsewhere. None the less, it was his dispensation to be an eminent though not a voluminous exponent of an altered conception of qualities in literature, and, in spite of his instinctive avoidance of the solemnities of "founding a school", his observations in criticism appear historically as part of a progressive theory, a movement—if we must have it against his affronted shade, the Romantic Movement. The marshals of this advance or deviation were, besides himself, Wordsworth, Coleridge, Southey, Hazlitt, T. N. Talfourd and Leigh Hunt, nor did each of these critics square his theories exactly with those of his neighbour; but their main harmony was none the worse for that.

What change or discovery did they make? One may almost say, that as critics they discovered or rediscovered the soul. They pointed out greatness or the want of it by an unfamiliar expectancy and delicacy of response to life and letters. Their manner of estimating genius was not to estimate it, in the former measurement of principles observed or neglected, but instead by an antiphonal beauty to transmit its effect on their spirits. They did not come forward as delegates of an academy of ordinances and precepts, as spokesmen for statutory common knowledge, but rather as personal, half-private judges, working in subtle discriminations which would not readily yield to methodical disquisition. An epigram of Coleridge's (though written on a physiologist) may illustrate their attitude towards superficial treatment of literature:

> O these facts! these facts!
> Of *such* facts I'm a-weary;

Light I can get none,
For all my eye is mere eye!
My eye and Betty Martin!
And that's a fact for sartain.

Their regard for what they read dwelt in the
total impression, or atmosphere, rather than the
detached appearance of one detail or another,
considered with little allowance for individual
unities. Their attitude, which was not entirely
free from false results, is that which mainly exists
at present. Before them, the stern word "cor-
rectness", which was not entirely bad in effect,
had had too much of the game.

Of the older criticism, there cannot be a better
example than Johnson, who died in time to be
spared the "modern cant", as I fear he would
have called it, of truth and beauty, or "that
intenseness of feeling, which seems to resolve
itself into the elements which it contemplates"
(Lamb's expression); I speak with deference to
the observant sympathy of Professor Nichol
Smith, who calls Johnson at once the "final exponent" of the older criticism, and one of the
leaders of the new. He points out that there is a
retrospective character in Johnson's "great preface to Shakespeare", a plain summary of authori-
tative opinions, a severe audit of Shakespeare's
"defects", but that when Johnson is at his ease

in the Notes, he is the herald of "the new subject—the study of Shakespeare's characters, and
the study of Shakespeare through his characters".
Professor Nichol Smith quotes his Johnson on
Polonius, on Falstaff: "But *Falstaff* unimitated,
unimitable *Falstaff*, how shall I describe thee?
Thou compound of sense and vice: of sense which
may be admired but not esteemed, of vice which
may be despised, but hardly detested...". There,
for a moment, we seem listening to Lamb fifty
years later. But, I would venture, the criticism
of Johnson even here is in the main explanatory,
not of total effect, but of certain characteristics;
his Falstaff is an odd sort of man rather than the
spirit of misrule. The pulse of the Doctor "tem-
perately keeps time", after an instant of gay
abandonment.

Apart from occasional articles and paragraphs,
Lamb began to publish his criticism in the year
1808, in the "Specimens of English Dramatic
Poets"; and characteristically he made no osten-
tation of what he offered there. His chief
business was to commend; he had done his dis-
commending by way of rejecting silently. His
method of commendation was the seemingly
simple one of catching the spirit of his authors
and speaking for them in the height of that
experience; songs of experience might be the

proper term for his notes. With a glad seriousness, and a solemn music, he declares the mysteries of genius; and he is never so enraptured
by one kind of achievement as not to perceive
another of a grander or a richer element. In a
world of dreams he finds his sure way. So, he
gives his discriminated impressions of the witches
of Thomas Middleton, and of those of Shakespeare, and while he utters a verdict he asserts
a new Middletonian and a new Shakespearean
province. Middleton's—"these are creatures to
whom man or woman, plotting some dire mis-
chief, might resort for occasional consultation".
Shakespeare's—"those originate deeds of blood,
and begin bad impulses to men. From the
moment that their eyes first meet with Macbeth's,
he is spell-bound. That meeting sways his destiny. He cannot break the fascination. These
witches can hurt the body, those have power
over the soul. Hecate in Middleton has a son,
a low buffoon: the hags of Shakespeare have
neither child of their own, nor seem to be descended from any parent. They are foul anomalies,
of whom we know not whence they are sprung,
nor whether they have beginning or ending....
But, in a lesser degree, the witches of Middleton
are fine creations. Their power too is, in some
measure, over the mind. They raise jars,

jealousies, strifes, 'like a thick scurf' over life".

Into this harmonizing of the criticism in its expression with the quality of the work criticized, Lamb has diverted that poetical art which in his earlier days gave his verse such sensitive light and shade. He portrays the intangible with fresh imagery, with personal emotion. "I never read it", he will say of a scene in Tourneur, "but my ears tingle, and I feel a hot blush overspread my cheeks, as if I were presently about to proclaim such malefactions of myself as the brothers here rebuke in their unnatural parent, in words more keen and dagger-like than those which Hamlet speaks to his mother." Alone with Webster (for who at that date had wrestled with that dark mind?), Lamb was at once right in his delimitation of the kingdom of that dramatist, and unique in his transfusion of Webster's deadly dogged note into his own sentences. The Duchess of Malfy, he shows, shares that automatic life which Coleridge imparts to the crew of the "Ancient Mariner". "She has lived among horrors till she is become 'native and endowed unto that element'. She speaks the dialect of despair; her tongue has a smatch of Tartarus and the souls in bale. To move a horror skilfully, to touch a soul to the quick, to lay upon

fear as much as it can bear, to wean and weary
a life till it is ready to drop, and then step in with
mortal instruments to take its last forfeit; this
only a Webster can do. Inferior geniuses may
'upon horror's head horrors accumulate', but
they cannot do this. They mistake quantity for
quality; they terrify 'babes with painted devils';
but they know not how a soul is to be moved.
Their terrors want dignity, their affrightments
are without decorum." And again he says: "The
sorrows of the Duchess set inward; if she talks,
it is little more than soliloquy imitating conversation in a kind of bravery". To my taste, such
brief essential words of Lamb's are criticism in
its most nervous and gifted kind, or condition;
he is called (deep calls to deep), and he answers
with sublimity. No poem is composed of phrase
and tone more subtly selected and ordered, more
curious and apt in the associations aroused; and
it may be urged that in these marginalia not
only are the faculties of vision and invention and
minor talents of literary form displayed, but also
the virtue of the original works is so distilled
into a "little room", that, were some future race
only to know Elizabethan drama through Lamb's
comments, they would be able to realize something of the peculiar magic of Ford's "Broken
Heart", and to scan the lost works as a moun-

tain-range in the crystal glass of this unassuming seer.

Here let me notice that Lamb and Coleridge alike excelled not only in critical delight but also in the poetical communication of it; the two could speak with one voice on the qualities of some of their favourite authors, as their two handwritings fill up the margins of some copies. You cannot always be sure (other evidence apart) which of them is the author of a beautiful little evocation or description of an old master. In their mutual friend Basil Montagu's "Selections from Taylor and Others" (the third edition, 1829), an example is found: this note on Sir Thomas Browne. "I wonder and admire his entireness in every subject that is before him. He follows it, he never wanders from it, and he has no occasion to wander; for whatever happens to be the subject, he metamorphoses all nature into it. In that treatise on some urns dug up in Norfolk, how earthly, how redolent of graves and sepulchres is every line! You have now dark mold, now a thigh bone, now a skull, then a bit of a mouldered coffin, a fragment of an old tombstone with moss in its 'Hic iacet', a ghost or a winding sheet, or the echo of a funeral psalm wafted on a November wind; and the gayest thing you shall meet with shall be a silver nail or a gilt 'Anno Domini', from a perished coffin top." To that passage, which appears like a typical landscape of an imaginative personality by Lamb, Montagu, who knew the two men and their works well, has added the initials C. L.; but the source of the piece is actually[1] a letter of Coleridge's. It would be possible to produce a volume of critical notes by Coleridge and by Lamb (excluding the examinations of theory which Coleridge undertook), as though by one writer; and that volume would be a succession of imagination and fancy illustrating fine judgment, in the way that poetry itself works.

Coleridge, in his "Table Talk", offers us as a "good gauge or criterion of genius,—whether it progresses and evolves, or only spins upon itself". He contrasts Dryden's satire with Pope's, and adds: "In like manner compare Charles Lamb's exquisite criticisms on Shakespeare with Hazlitt's round and round imitations of them". —He was talking twenty years or more after Lamb's first emerging among the few whose fortunate part it has been to add even a few words to the Shakespeare we know. For the

[1] This was pointed out to me by Mr Frederick Page, and I seize the occasion of mentioning his name in order to add that he has annotated "The Last Essays of Elia" with distinguished skill and fidelity.

opportunity, he was indebted to that remarkable pair of reformist brothers, John and Leigh
Hunt, who had in 1808 established their Sunday
newspaper, *The Examiner*, with the object of
freshening and creating conscience, taste and
activity in many fields of England's interest, from
army flogging to architecture. Immediately succeeding in this liberal project, they presently
conceived what was not yet a familiar notion,
that of a quarterly magazine; and *The Reflector* of 1810 and 1811 came into existence.
It had one unusual starting-point (like *Knight's
Quarterly Magazine* some years after): most of
the contributors had been educated at one school.
Among these Lamb was the chief. Not to mention a good many of his levities and whimsical
papers, *The Reflector* was the means of his
publishing two essays of a more elaborate criticism than he had previously completed. The first
was "On the Genius of Hogarth", the second
"On Garrick and Acting, and the Plays of
Shakespeare, considered with reference to their
fitness for Stage Representation"; this latter
being No. 1 of an intended series of "Theatra-
lia". The demise of *The Reflector* from want
of capital cut short the intention; yet the mis-
fortune had some relief, for the magazine, so far
forming only two middle-sized volumes, was

republished as a book or miscellany, and what Lamb had printed in it was accordingly saved from partial inaccessibility.

The essay on Hogarth had its very beginnings, as Lamb at once recalls in its exordium, in the old house in Hertfordshire, where the prints of the Rake's and the Harlot's Progress had seemed to the wise child not to be things to laugh at but potent tragic narrative. It was in defence and promotion of this way of reading Hogarth that Lamb took his mature view of Hogarth as a whole; and he did not escape the feeling that he was speaking for the few against the many, broad laughter being more popular than the central and the outlying themes of beauty and truth. Out of the sphere of the Bunburys and the Gillrays even, Lamb came to raise the fame of Hogarth as high as "the best comedy exceeds the best farce that ever was written", or rather to show his genius in the light of that which created Timon and Lear. The eloquent prose gives us still, what it taught Lamb's generation, the comprehension of Hogarth's prodigious abundance of human knowledge, and the force of argument which dwelt within and which controlled that multitudinous sea of significant circumstance. To quote from such sustained and interwoven criticism, where so many parentheses

develop the case precisely as far as the author
meant, is to convey an imperfect impression, and
suggest a solid unyielding manifesto; but the
style is worth a glance, for it has been a light
to the age between. Lamb takes that print of
"Gin Lane", and Poussin's "Plague of Athens".
He begs us to regard the one as though its age
and locality were like those of the other, and
not as something just round the corner of the
Tottenham Court Road; he asks us to consider
not the inferior externals of an engraving con-
trasted with the picture's colour, but the matter
for mind and spirit symbolized. He then declares
for "Gin Lane". "There is more of imagination
in it—that power which draws all things to one,
—which makes things animate and inanimate,
beings with their attributes, subjects and their
accessaries, take one colour, and serve to one
effect. Every thing in the print, to use a vulgar
expression, *tells*. Every part is full of 'strange
images of death'. It is perfectly amazing and
astounding to look at. Not only the two prominent figures, the woman and the half-dead
man, which are as terrible as any thing which
Michael Angelo ever drew, but every thing else
in the print contributes to bewilder and stupefy,
—the very houses, as I heard a friend of mine
express it, tumbling all about in various directions,

seem drunk—seem absolutely reeling from the effect of that diabolical spirit of phrenzy which goes forth over the whole composition." And, as he urges this example of imaginative congruousness or congress, he suddenly seems showing us equally why Wordsworth's sonnet upon Westminster Bridge has from its first publication spell-bound us, though there "the very houses seem asleep". To pursue Lamb further in his revelation of the art of "a clear light", I give the next passage, "one little circumstance". Hogarth is not easily shut in. "Not content with the dying and dead figures, which he has strewn in profusion over the proper scene of the action, he shows you what (of a kindred nature) is passing beyond it. Close by the shell, in which, by direction of the parish beadle, a man is depositing his wife, is an old wall, which, partaking of the universal decay around it, is tumbling to pieces. Through a gap in this wall are seen three figures, which appear to make a part in some funeral procession which is passing by on the other side of the wall, out of the sphere of the composition....*Imaginary work*, where the spectator must meet the artist in his conceptions half way; and it is peculiar to the confidence of high genius alone to trust so much to spectators or readers."

Such writings were the embodiment of a new apprehension of the capacity of the human being, the rights of man in imaginative adventure. "What a piece of worke is a man! how Noble in Reason? how infinite in faculty? in forme and mouing how expresse and admirable? in Action, how like an Angel? in apprehension, how like a God?"—it is in this consciousness of Hamlet's that the critics Lamb and Coleridge, Hazlitt and Hunt, applied themselves to great subjects. Or I would transfer the words of Emily Brontë from the mystical to the psychological: "Strange Power, I trust thy might". If Lamb showed this glory in man's range and invention through his interpreting of Hogarth, he did so with even more of beauty's passion in the essay on Shakespeare's tragedies. The upshot, and as some say the heresy, of that essay is that "Lear [he means the character of Lear] is essentially impossible to be represented on a stage". I remember Mr Hardy saying the same thing independently of Lamb; that great drama was only possible to the reader sitting by the fire. Lamb also adds other instances, and concludes by declaring that not the tragic "essences" alone are beyond the actual theatre but that your comic heroes, your Falstaff and Shallow, are so. Supposing that he were wrong in this, of what description would the error be? Not that which makes

>learned commentators view
>In Homer more than Homer knew,

but that of a too romantic mind, always transforming the common and substantial into something rich and strange; which should be no deplorable fault. In the essay, he informs us whence his feeling on the subject took its course; and once again, he went back to boyhood, and the first time he saw a tragedy of Shakespeare, and the "very high degree of satisfaction" he then had. But, he adds, he had soon paid in his feelings for that mundane exhibition of what had been something without limits; "a fine vision" had been "brought down to the standard of flesh and blood".

And so he enquired into the nature of his disappointment. He discusses very skilfully the conventions of actors, audiences, managers; the crudity of much stage treatment of passages with undercurrents of relationship or attitude more important to be mastered than the surface words; but his mighty contention was that Shakespeare's creations were for the mind, not the eye and ear. His central figure in this thesis is of course Lear, and he fights for the sublimity of that personage with a formidable metaphor. "The greatness of Lear is not in corporal dimension, but in intellectual: the explosions of his passion are as terrible as a vòlcano: they are storms turning up and disclosing to the bottom that sea, his mind, with all its vast riches. It is his mind which is laid bare. This case of flesh and blood seems too insignificant to be thought on; even as he himself neglects it. On the stage we see nothing but corporal infirmities and weakness, the impotence of rage; while we read it, we see not Lear, but we are Lear,—we are in his mind, we are sustained by a grandeur which baffles the malice of daughters and storms; in the aberrations of his reason, we discover a mighty irregular power of reasoning, immethodized from the ordinary purposes of life, but exerting its powers, as the wind blows where it listeth, at will upon the corruptions and abuses of mankind. What have looks, or tones, to do with that sublime identification of his age with that of the *heavens themselves*, when in his reproaches to them for conniving at the injustice of his children, he reminds them that 'they themselves are old'? What gesture shall we appropriate to this?" There is, I suspect, never an answer. That mind confronting the creative abyss will not be schooled into a voice, a pointing hand; no white beard will tell the eternities of that experience; yet, supposing again that Lamb were in error, his vindication is not hard. He has made us think ever more deeply over the purposes of Shakespeare, the integrity of Shakespeare's own text, the art of putting his plays on the stage and of representing all that is possible of those characters who, at every reading, seem to have a new turn of meaning in something that is given them to speak.

So, in a short time and a narrow compass, Lamb had proved himself the most perceptive, bold and appropriate critic of Shakespeare and his contemporaries who had yet spoken; for not even Coleridge, lecturing in 1808 and again in 1810 and 1811, had presented the old drama with such fullness of reading and finished utterance. It is the greatest pity that Lamb's next important critical study—of Wordsworth's poetry, in "The Excursion"—comes down to us mangled, "vulgarized and frozen" by the editor of *The Quarterly Review*. Lamb's annoyance with Wordsworth's very strong sense of *his* high calling was over; he had measured his man, and given up the notion of mutual understanding as he wished it; he submitted himself modestly to the genius that he recognized, out-topping the personal. Even his anger at the ruining of his

carefully composed review was rather because
he had been baulked of playing his part in the
recommendation of a masterly poet than because
his own quality had been so rudely mauled.

The suspected incompleteness of our present
list of Lamb's writings must be particularly
taken into account in a notice of his critical work.
For example, from January 1815 to November
1818 no contribution by him to a newspaper or
review is traced; and yet the general evidence
of the list goes to show that he was very partial
to occasional journalism. We do not know
enough of him as a critic in print of his eminent
contemporaries. Two or three years ago, the
manuscript of a long and perfectly written review of Hazlitt's Table Talk, by Lamb, passed
through the sale-rooms; it was supposed to be
unpublished, and has not been published since
it appeared and disappeared. It is likely that
it had been printed in a journal in Lamb's time,
—and was an instance of what has not been
identified. I must think it strange if Lamb never
took the chance of welcoming in a public manner
such works of Coleridge as the "Biographia
Literaria" or "Sibylline Leaves", not to mention
other writers for whom he would have had a
double friendship—that of acquaintance and that
of literary zeal. It is strange that in 1820 Lamb

is found suddenly, once, as a reviewer for the
New Times (his next known articles in it are
six years later); and this isolated review honours
a young poet, John Keats. It is worth while to
see the method which Lamb chose in order to
pay as valuable and influential a tribute as he
could to the "Lamia" volume. He began by
transcribing two or three of the most harmonious
and splendid stanzas of the " Eve of Saint Agnes ",
then straight from the press, not inscribed on
everybody's remembrance; the first line of his
prelude of beauty was "A casement high and
triple-arched there was", the last "As though
a rose should shut, and be a bud again". He
went on to compare the radiance of Keats's
genius, "the almost Chaucer-like painting" to
that illumining brightness which shone through
the casement to glorify the kneeling Madeline; and
with one touch he suggested the relationship of
this man's romantic delicacy with "Christabel."
This was something of a beginning. But he proceeded: "The finest thing in the volume is the
paraphrase of Boccaccio's story of the Pot of
Basil". He told the story briefly, touching in
by the way the wonderful conception in one
epithet:

> So the two brothers and their *murder'd* man
>   Rode past fair Florence;

repeating the stanzas in which is described
Isabella's digging out her lover's body, and
calling them equal for diction, outline and
sentiment to anything in Dante, in Chaucer,
in Spenser. One would think he knew all
Keats's private reading, for those were his
special authors. And still Lamb expands his
praise. "More exuberantly rich in imagery and
painting is the story of the Lamia. It is of as
gorgeous stuff as ever romance was composed
of." Referring to "these prodigal phrases which
Mr Keats abounds in, which are each a poem in
a word", Lamb flashes across the imagination
his swift series of fantasies derived from the
poem. And then, he reverts, not claiming to
preach to Keats, but adhering to his own preference: "Lamia" is "for younger impressi-
bilities. To us an ounce of feeling is worth a
pound of fancy; and therefore we recur again,
with a warmer gratitude, to the story of Isabella
and the pot of basil, and those never-cloying
stanzas which we have cited, and which we think
should disarm criticism, if it be not in its nature
cruel; if it would not deny to honey its sweetness,
nor to roses redness, nor light to the stars in
Heaven; if it would not bay the moon out of the
skies, rather than acknowledge she is fair". This
review, for the recovery of which we must thank

Mr E. V. Lucas, above all his finds, has always affected me powerfully; in skill of arrangement, in immediate and prophetic recognition, in frequent and congenial suggestion and allusion; but above all the closing sentence reflects, with its perfect and unlaboured imagery, the brilliant immortality of Keats's poetical presence, and the miserable shadow of his detractors dies away from the elemental sweetness and light.

Lamb was very willing to repeat and to eulogize the poetry of Keats to his private friends; more than one[1] record of that exists; it is even

[1] For example, in a review of Willis's "Pencillings", *Gentleman's Magazine*, March 1836: "The most pleasing of Keats's poems is one that Mr Willis has not mentioned, viz. 'The Eve of St Agnes'. We once sate discoursing on this 'pretty jewel' with Charles Lamb, at his villa at Islington, till all our goodly flasks and flagons were void; and when the watchman called four in the morning, we tripped back to London with the fresh and rosy Hornsey milkmaids, looking very like one of the prints in Walton's Angler; so be it known, on our authority, that Charles Lamb considered this poem to be 'of good conceit and well handled, and the counterfeit action very lively and pleasant, keeping the staffe of seven and the verse of ten'." See also Leigh Hunt's "Lord Byron", 1828, 2nd ed., I, 427, and Barry Cornwall's memoir of Lamb, 1866, p. 222.

better known that he had no regard for Shelley's
work. Shelley, admiring Lamb much, regretfully
ascribed his failure to make friends with him to
the "calumny of an enemy"; and it is possible
that, alike with Shelley and with Byron, Lamb,
scrupulous in his system of conduct, permitted
moral indignation to disturb his literary appreciation. The extraordinary manner in which he
had subjected his own genius to the burden of a
selfless life probably caused him to condemn men
who seemed to claim for their genius a wild
irregularity in humanities more urgent than even
verse. However, Lamb's pleasure in a crystal-
clear style and a paradox made him copy out in his
common-place book, and commend to his friends
with "Pray like it very much", one little poem
of Shelley's, to a Reviewer,

> —Of your antipathy
> If I am the Narcissus, you are free
> To pine into a sound with hating me.

And, what is more surprising, Lamb admired
"The Cenci"! The common-place books of
Lamb tell us something about his admirations
which his collected writings do not; there we
see him deep in the direct wonder of the old
ballads, in Elizabethan and also Stuart lyrical
poetry; there he preserves, because of the "grace

without a name", such lucky pieces as Barry
Cornwall's

> Sing, who sings
> To her who wears a hundred rings?—

as Fitzgerald's "The Meadows in Spring"—
"'Tis a dull sight to see the old year dying",
as Hamilton Reynolds's sonnets to Robin Hood.
There too Lamb selects from Smart's "Song to
David", a song to which hardly anybody listened
for about a century and a half, and now offered
to the million in the series of "Augustan Poets"
and half-a-dozen other forms. From other sources
it is known that Lamb found extreme happiness
in Landor's "Rose Aylmer", and in those poems
of John Clare which flowed along in the vein of
Dyer's "Grongar Hill"; and indeed he was for
ever alert to fresh music and picture of prose
and verse, if he commonly avoided the ambitious
schemes of thought and creed, and the labyrinths
of fiction, which multiplied throughout his life-
time. Perhaps his personal acquaintance with
Godwin and Coleridge made him more than
naturally shy of philosophical arguments.

From time to time Lamb wrote a theatrical
critique, his interest being rather in the talents
and characteristics of the actors than in the pieces
which they performed; he indeed seems to have

preferred to see plays competent rather than conspicuous, plays which were not beyond the performers either way. He delighted in the problems of acting and the art and spirit, every smile and every tear, with which his favourites could conquer them. For years he had especially watched Fanny Kelly, whose best parts were those of simple life and manners; he had published a sonnet to her, without his name—but his friends had no trouble in ascribing it—so early as 1813; in 1819 he saw her as a gipsy in Richard Brome's "Jovial Crew", and what he wrote, or part of it, will show vividly the sympathetic study of actors of genius which he was pioneer in. "Her gabbling lachrymose petitions; her tones, such as we have heard by the side of old woods, when an irresistible face has come peeping on one on a sudden; with her full black locks, and a *voice*— how shall we describe it? a voice that was by nature meant to convey nothing but truth and goodness, but warped by circumstance into an assurance that she is telling us a lie—that catching twitch of the thievish irreproveable finger—those ballad-singers' notes, so vulgar yet so unvulgar—that assurance, so like impudence, and yet so many countless leagues removed from it—her jeers, which we had rather stand, than be caressed with other ladies' compliments, a summer's day long—her face, with a wild out-of-doors grace upon it—." This is the same faculty of inspired response and representative appreciation that yield's Lamb's criticism of great literature; the same exaltation in the innumerable delicacies and ranges of the gifted human being; and we may say that through his dithyramb and its essential creations we have *seen* Miss Kelly in Brome's "Jovial Crew", more distinctly, more vitally than the actresses we have seen this winter on the stage itself.

"But what have we to gain by praising Miss Kelly?" Those words also are Lamb's, and part of a dramatic criticism written a month later than the other. Small wonder that he had been at his best in praising her, in perpetuating her transient perfection; for he was in love with her. I need not tell once more the story of his proposal, her refusal—so choice and pretty, and yet so painful to one who guesses the depths of Lamb's life; it was all begun and ended between the writing of these criticisms. Many years of silence had spoken; there was nothing more to say; and Lamb went on praising Miss Kelly in his occasional duty of dramatic criticism.

Meanwhile, in 1818, the two small volumes entitled "The Works of Charles Lamb" had appeared, their contents being gathered by the diligence of friends rather than by any effort of Lamb's,—and old newspapers, once lost, are difficult to replace. The "Works" contained a few pieces of prose and verse which are not known to have been printed before, and I shall be pardoned if I break the exact sequence of my chapter here, by way of refreshment, with the sonnet To Miss Kelly—poetic criticism.

You are not, Kelly, of the common strain
That stoop their pride and female honor down
To please that many-headed beast *the town,*
And vend their lavish smiles and tricks for gain;
By fortune thrown amid the actors' train
You keep your native dignity of thought;
The plaudits that attend you come unsought
As tributes due unto your natural vein.
Your tears have passion in them, and a grace
Of genuine freshness, which our hearts avow;
Your smiles are winds whose ways we cannot trace,
That vanish and return we know not how—
And please the better from a pensive face,
A thoughtful eye, and a reflecting brow.

The "Works" contained, besides the magnificent Hogarth and Shakespeare interpretations, a short study of George Wither's poetry, which has been very useful to that poet and his readers; but its characteristics need no defining now. I leave the subject of Lamb's critical work at about

the year 1819, to resume it necessarily from
time to time in the subsequent sketches of his
genius; for he had still to write several glorious
pages, on authors, on painters, on actors, and
on the principles of all their arts. He had already
achieved a new criticism, which has been more
often resorted to and borrowed from than the
mass of speculation and proposition produced
by his friends, not because of its superiority in
idea, but of its beauty of expression as well as
its idea. He remained an incidental critic, un-
aspiring even in the day of his success; and,
much as we should have valued a book of
regular, comprehensive critical theory from
Lamb, he was the best judge of his vocation.
He chose, in general, to hold his peace as any
sort of authority unless some impulse chiefly
lyrical, some cause which attracted him singu-
larly and which he could affect with his matured
and spirited opinions, were to compel him to
speak. Mr Tillyard has gathered his literary
criticism into a volume which is in a way—in a
comparison with what might have been—a thing
of shreds and patches; but above those detached
thoughts the editor has inscribed the fairest
things, and one especially—"quintessential criticism". Had Lamb been living in our time, it
might be that he would have gone with the time;

he would certainly have been invited to write a thousand more reviews, a score more volumes of appreciation, than he did; he would have been delivering this series of lectures, I fancy. What beauties of thought co-natural with feeling, of phrase co-sphered with both he would have stammered out! But Lamb was a clerk of the India House; he only made one speech that we hear of, and that ended after the one word "Gentlemen"; he lived before a newspaper had featured —I think they call it—a symposium of reluctant opinions by authors on their favourite footwear or the next life; and no instance is tabulated of his having supplied an introduction to a book on the art of writing or the future of the talkies.

CHAPTER V

ALMOST PERFECT
SYMPATHIES

It has been the inevitable argument of this sketch that Lamb was greater even than his writings, those being temporary admissions to parts of his private mind, not exhaustive extraordinary inspirations, such as concentrate not only their authors' faculties but a great deal that did not belong to them before and will not again. Along this line lies the explanation of the preference which many have for Lamb's letters over his published works; and more fully it would appear that Lamb himself sitting and consulting impressed his friends even more deeply than by essay or by letter. When Leigh Hunt observes that "Charles Lamb had a head worthy of Aristotle", it is clear that the conception of Elia had fallen short of his occasion, and that a sense of a really masterly intellect alone had the last word. A short acquaintance with Lamb was enough to arouse a similar opinion in almost

everybody. Mr Alaric "Attila" Watts, for instance, who was not altogether pleased with
Lamb's bearing, and is one of the less engaging
critics of that day, must address a poem to the
author of essays, beginning,

Quaint masker! why hide, 'neath a garb so uncouth,
A well-spring of song, and a day-star of truth?
Why struggle, to bury a heart-cherished brood
Of fine fancies and feelings, in crambo so rude?

It has been noted how, to Lamb, a certain individual listener was essential, a Manning, a
Robert Lloyd, a Hazlitt, in order to produce from
him a triumphant and audacious symphony of
thought and word, "some passion that moves
him strongly". The irreverent have supposed
that Coleridge had Lamb particularly in his
mind's eye when he made the remark that some
men are like the musical glasses—in order to
bring from them their finest lines you have to
keep them wet. And I do not find that Coleridge
added any moral indignation. It is too curious
a complexity, this mystery called genius, to be
treated with copy-book maxims; the question is
what has to be removed before and in order that
the power may wake with joy and fearlessness,
and by what means the liberation may be accomplished. To some, perhaps turning on a gramo-
phone; to others, like Keats, perhaps dressing

up and adonizing as if to go out, and then sitting down to write; to others, the rain and wind; to others, one countenance, one footstep; to others, perfumes recaptured; and why not to some, monotony's or time's victims, the aid of their glass?

Lamb has been mightily abused as an instance of intemperance; the latest and largest biography of Carlyle carries on the tradition grimly. But then, he himself published in 1813 that strange essay the "Confessions of a Drunkard"—he republished it in 1822 with Elia's signature. In that piece of writing (contributed to "The Philanthropist", which alone tells us something of the intention), "the weak, the nervous" are addressed; "those who feel the want of some artificial aid to raise their spirits in society to what is no more than the ordinary pitch of all around them without it". The point in view is the danger and final fallacy of such unfortunate characters, if they resort to strong liquors; "Reader, if you are gifted with nerves like mine, aspire to any character but that of a wit. When you find a tickling relish upon your tongue disposing you to that sort of conversation, especially if you find a preternatural flow of ideas setting in upon you at the sight of a bottle and fresh glasses, avoid giving way to it as you would fly your certain destruction. If you cannot crush the power of fancy, or that within you which you mistake for such, divert it, give it some other play. Write an essay, pen a character or description,—but not as I do now, with tears trickling down your cheeks". I am not so much concerned with the object of Lamb's "Confessions" as the revelation that they yield of his inner conflict, his extreme openness to nervous tortures. The essay shifts from the humorous to the terrible; even tobacco becomes a kind of dancing devil, not the fair shape that Sir James Barrie has drawn, nor the valuable friendliness that made Spurgeon in the vestry say, "I smoke to the glory of God"; no, but a cunning incubus. Drinking is presented with still keener fantasy of "dreadful truth". Lamb projects himself, or is projected, into a dizzy chasm, of which the copious records of his life do not afford the evidence. Here we may best discover what dragons he had to quell, what ghosts to lay, before he could be the happy and the wise philosopher of a great many friends.

The pure heights to which Lamb could lead his friends, once away from his Tartarus, as he calls these figments, scruples, black thoughts, illusions of his own, are illustrated by Hazlitt's essay "On Persons whom One would Wish to have Seen"; but I shall consult some of the other observers, those who kept up the custom of expressing friendship in verse. In early days, Coleridge drew the portrait of Lamb in his finest spirits (though not in London): kept at home while Lamb and others went for their walk, Coleridge perceived what Lamb was:

> Now my friends emerge
> Beneath the wide wide heaven—and view again
> The many-steepled tract magnificent
> Of hilly fields and meadows, and the sea,
> With some fair bark, perhaps, whose sails light up
> The slip of smooth clear blue betwixt two Isles
> Of purple shadow! Yes! they wander on
> In gladness all; but thou, methinks, most glad,
> My gentle-hearted Charles! for thou hast pined
> And hunger'd after Nature, many a year,
> In the great City pent, winning thy way
> With sad yet patient soul, through evil and pain
> And strange calamity! Ah! slowly sink
> Behind the Western ridge, thou glorious Sun!
> Shine in the slant beams of the sinking orb,
> Ye purple heath-flowers! richlier burn, ye clouds!
> Live in the yellow light, ye distant groves!
> And kindle, thou blue Ocean! so my friend
> Struck with deep joy may stand, as I have stood,
> Silent with swimming sense; yea, gazing round,
> On the wide landscape, gaze till all doth seem
> Less gross than bodily; and of such hues

As veil the Almighty Spirit, when yet he makes
Spirits perceive his presence.
                A delight
Comes sudden on my heart, and I am glad
As I myself were there!

The passage is all a vision of the appropriateness
of these beautiful forms to the spirit of Lamb;
but especially in those last words do we become
aware of the radiance that Lamb cast on the
mind of his illustrious friend. For a moment, all
fumbling estimate and agreeable anecdote vanished into a simple rapture that the sweet yet
sublime soul had found a heavenly interval and
air. Yet Coleridge's exalted portrait had in it
that which upset Lamb, and drew from him
two letters which, while they secretly insisted on
a still closer comprehension, were at the moment
a sign of imperfect sympathy: "In the next
edition, please to blot out 'gentle-hearted'"
(Coleridge has repeated it three times) "and
substitute drunken-dog, ragged-head, odd-eyed,
stuttering or any other epithet which truly and
properly belongs to the gentleman in question.
And for Charles read Tom, or Bob, or Richard,
for more delicacy. Damn you, I was beginning
to forgive you and believe in earnest that the
lugging in of my proper name was purely un-
intentional on your part, when looking back for

further conviction, stares me in the face *Charles Lamb of the India House. Now* I am convinced it was all done in malice, heaped sack-upon-sack, congregated, studied malice. You Dog! your 141st page shall not save you. I own I was just ready to acknowledge that there is a something not unlike good poetry in that page, if you had not run into the unintelligible abstraction-fit about the manner of the Deity's making spirits perceive his presence. God, nor created thing alive, can receive any honour from such thin show-box attributes".

But what had excited such vehemence? In great part, a religious humility, which Lamb reserved from the knowledge of his friends almost entirely—but it came out upon any allusion to the Creator that seemed to profess information, and profane the illimitable with anthropomorphic figures. Coleridge coined the phrase of "the bowéd mind", Lamb had that mind. The question of "gentle-hearted" was a secondary irritation, —secondary, but considerable; for Lamb was not in the mood to saint himself, and would have bitten Thackeray for sainting him later. Then, too, he was well aware how easily a balanced and restrained humanity, such as he strove to perfect, would be misunderstood into limpness or unrealism. "For God's sake (I never was more serious), don't make me ridiculous any more by terming me gentle-hearted in print, or do it in better verses. It did well enough five years ago when I came to see you, and was moral coxcomb enough at the time you wrote the lines, to feed upon such epithets; but, besides that the meaning of gentle is equivocal at best, and almost always means poor-spirited, the very quality of gentleness is abhorrent to such vile trumpetings. My *sentiment* is long since vanished. I hope my *virtues* have done *sucking*. I can scarce think but you meant it in joke. I hope you did, for I should be ashamed to think that you could think to gratify me by such praise, fit only to be a cordial to some green-sick sonnetteer." This was written before Lamb had quite emerged from the supposition that in men of greater creative abilities he would find his own nature fully and delicately comprehended, and is of a piece with his ironical postscript to Wordsworth, "Thank you for Liking my Play!" He gave up the hope that he should be understood, and went to his grave with the distinction that he had compassed Coleridge's and Wordsworth's character and genius but that they had never mastered his mystery. What had been bitter remained only as a fact in human variety.

Coleridge did not expunge that word "gentle"

from the poem, nor indeed did he give it up as adequate to Lamb's general value and conduct. "Nothing", he said thirty years later, "ever left a stain on that gentle creature's mind, which looked upon the degraded men and things around him like moonshine on a dunghill, which shines and takes no pollution. All things are shadows to him, except those which move his affections." Wordsworth found no difficulty in keeping the term; in November 1835 he lamented that

> Lamb, the frolic and the gentle
> Had vanished from our lonely hearth,

and the same year, in the lines "Written After the Death of Charles Lamb", he pointed out that

> From the most gentle creature nursed in fields
> Had been derived the name he bore.

But I should do amiss to treat Wordsworth's elegy on Lamb with frivolity. It is agreed that it did not serve the purpose for which it was requested, namely, to be inscribed on Lamb's headstone; indeed, mathematicians have computed the mighty area of marble which the 130 lines of blank verse would occupy, and Wordsworth himself observed the discrepancy, after writing the first 38 lines. "That aim is missed"; but we are the gainers by the failure of Words-

worth in the epitaph line. For his poem is of a
lofty and a glorious kind, plain though the language is; and he does express the *altitudo* of
Lamb's personality and influence far more
thoughtfully than a host of subsequent writers
to whom Lamb's outwall with its Punch and
Judy shows and all the fun of the fair has been
the principal thing to report. Wordsworth, of
course, did not forget that Lamb had occasionally
lapsed into a certain insubordination; but he was
gracious in the summing-up:

> And if in him meekness at times gave way,
> Provoked out of herself by troubles strange,
> Many and strange, that hung about his life;
> Still, at the centre of his being, lodged
> A soul by resignation sanctified:
> And if too often, self-reproached, he felt
> That innocence belongs not to our kind,
> A power that never ceased to abide in him,
> Charity, 'mid the multitude of sins
> That she can cover, left not his expos'd
> To an unforgiving judgment from just Heaven.
> O, he was good, if e'er a good Man lived!

And suddenly Wordsworth, like Coleridge in
that earlier poem, became aware of something
more in Lamb than what the word "gentle",
the word "good" conveys; some universal light
and unity, an inspiration, "a grace without a

name ". He resumed his poem not as an epitaph but as a song of honour:

> Thou wert a scorner of the fields, my Friend,
> But more in show than truth; and from the fields,
> And from the mountains, to thy rural grave
> Transported, my soothed spirit hovers o'er
> Its green untrodden turf, and blowing flowers....

Why so transported? The general charm, the magnetism resolved itself then into an explanation; there was a definite reason in this spiritual pilgrimage; Lamb had offered the theme of his devotion to Mary,

> that fraternal love, whose heaven-lit lamp
> From infancy, through manhood, to the last
> Of threescore years, and to thy latest hour,
> Burnt on with ever-strengthening light, enshrined
> Within thy bosom.

There Wordsworth was on sure ground, but even yet Lamb had slipped beyond his observation and interpreting.

We would find, if we could, Lamb's theory of this life and its government, and in what manner he regarded the attempts of his race to approach the deity. In his earlier years, he had been almost hermit-like in some moods, and had uttered his lonely hymn to godhead:

Mystery of God! thou brave and beauteous world,
Made fair with light and shade and stars and flowers,

Made fearful and august with woods and rocks,
Jagg'd precipice, black mountain, sea in storms;

but later on it becomes more difficult to find
him openly contemplating the seen and the un-
seen together. We know well enough that he was
a Unitarian; we may collect from his writings
that he honoured all sincere forms of worship,
and the attitude of devotion and of aspiration
wherever found. He went into more churches
than many churchmen, and invited us, in a
beautiful reverie, to "retire with him into a
Quaker's Meeting", whence, while he makes no
attempt at mystical passages towards the "Judge
of Spirits", he says we shall "go away with a
sermon not made with hands." But again we
find him as a consecrated spirit, with the "Lives
of the Saints" in his hands (you would not
perhaps have looked for him at a "Catholic
book-shop in Duke Street"); and in that seventeenth-century quarto at home he has discovered
a painted flower inserted, which at length opening proves to be "the cover to a very humble
draught of a St Anne, with the Virgin and Child;
doubtless the performance of some poor, but
pious Catholic, whose meditations it assisted."
Who then is happy but Lamb, as he writes (it is
towards his last days) his beautiful plain sonnet
on the significance: "O lift with reverent hand

that tarnish'd flower", the shrine, he says, that opened hints of "all Heaven" to the sense of one long ago. The book is extant, and the painted flower, to bear on the double piety of the former possessors. Then, too, let me think of Lamb's vigorous confidence in the maligned Scotch minister Edward Irving (set it against the attack on Irving's countrymen in Elia's "Imperfect Sympathies"); "firm, outspeaking, intrepid and docile as a pupil of Pythagoras"; let me peep at him, on occasion, "drinking tea in company with two Methodist divines of different persuasions, whom it was my fortune to introduce to each other". These are only scattered and broken relics; but do they not testify that Lamb had his own mysterious and many-flowered altar?

On one day at least he was moved to tell everybody that he was something more subtle than poor Yorick, or the little man who wrote the gay reckless rhymes on the Regent (people often took them to be Byron's). It was when his friend Southey, that biped Rectitude, had alluded to the Essays of Elia as "a book, which wants only a sounder religious feeling to be as delightful as it is original". It would not have disturbed Lamb much to find that even Southey did not particularly value his literary talent, but this casual invasion of a deep secluded place in his soul made him rise with the indignant swift power of a satirist. He asked the Reviewer whence the charge of heresy could have sprung among Elia's lucubrations; from the "paper on 'Saying Graces'", which was all for grace, or that on the "New Year", where natural feelings on death and severance from "this green earth" were spoken? "If men would honestly confess their misgivings (which few men will) there are times when the strongest Christians of us, I believe, have reeled under questionings of such staggering obscurity. I do not accuse you of this weakness. There are some who tremblingly reach out shaking hands to the guidance of Faith—Others who stoutly venture into the dark (their Human Confidence their leader, whom they mistake for Faith); and, investing themselves beforehand with Cherubic wings, as they fancy, find their new robes as familiar, and fitting to their supposed growth and stature in godliness, as the coat they left off yesterday— Some whose hope totters upon crutches—Others who stalk into futurity upon stilts." The Letter, with its song of honour, of wise gratefulness to the author of "this good world, which [man] knows, which was created so lovely, beyond his deservings", its modesty about the indefinite which

none the less seems reflected fair in that thanks-
giving, with its profusion of unerring glances at
theological systems, will remind us that Lamb
might,—by his education should—have been a
clergyman. His sermons[1] would have been remembered. I think I see him, in the seventeenth
century, a famous priest at Douai, or, as he
writes it, "St Omer's". But, as it was, he quietly
opened the doors of many places of worship,
tiptoed in and out again like Hartley Coleridge,
and was one with the world's highest sense, or
song. I emphasize even the literal side of this,
for not long since, when a paper on the clerks
of city churches was ascribed to Lamb, one
authority was rash enough to affirm that we did
not know of Lamb's ever attending a Church of
England service. The Letter to Southey, the
historian of that Church, answers. "The last time
I was in any of your places of worship was on

[1] When Mr E. S. Robertson visited Edmonton
in 1880 he was guided to Lamb's grave by an old
man who still spoke "of *Mr* Lamb. He went re-
gularly to church, said my informant, and the simple
village joke was, that the vicar was very friendly
with Lamb because he often wrote his sermons for
him. This piece of gossip at any rate indicates that
the vicar was on good terms with our dear Samaritan."
But was it only a joke? I fancy not.

Easter Sunday last. I had the satisfaction of listening to a very sensible sermon of an argumentative turn, delivered with great propriety, by one of your bishops. The place was Westminster Abbey."

I cannot omit to indicate other records which state to us the keenness of Lamb (the gentle) in controversial positions between sects, and in faiths and forms. Because he was a Unitarian, he had no intention of breaking down the carved work of the Established Church; so far from it that he was stirred to pen and to publish a letter to a friend of his own persuasion newly married, condemning an inconsistency. Congratulating him, he proceeds: "It was with pain I found you, after the ceremony, depositing in the vestry-room what is called a Protest. I thought you superior to this little sophistry....They do not force you into their Churches. You come voluntarily, knowing the terms. You marry in the name of the Trinity. There is no evading this by pretending that you take the formula with your own interpretation, (and so long as you can do this, where is the necessity of Protesting?): for the meaning of a vow is to be settled by the sense of the imposer, not by any forced construction of the taker....You marry then essentially as Trinitarians; and the altar no sooner satisfied than, hey presto, with the celerity of a juggler, you shift habits, and proceed pure Unitarians again in the vestry. You cheat the Church out of a wife, and go home smiling in your sleeves that you have so cunningly despoiled the Egyptians." Lamb went on to rebuke the insult to the minister whose benefit given had the result of his being harried with "these papers", and to sketch the history of dissent and tolerance; but his meaning throughout was larger than these details. He challenged the Unitarians to show a courage which would not be definable in "the smooth two-sided velvet of a Protesting Occasional Conformity". In another manner, the artfully learned essay "On the Religion of Actors" affords a proof that Lamb was expert in points of doctrine; and again his mastery of those is not the culmination of his spiritual life but one of the preparatory passages by which he had ventured into his own infinite reverence. I see that I have fallen on the same phrase there as his friend and biographer Procter employs.

The letter to Southey informs us of something besides Lamb's *religio laici*; it is his *de amicitia*, and he seizes the opportunity to reply to Southey (and perhaps to Wordsworth, who was not to be satisfied on this head) on the insinuation that he Lamb was better than the company he kept.

We have thus an intimate picture of a man
exquisite in understanding why he made friends,
which we might contrast with the spectacle of
Leigh Hunt in the same circle, not less affectionate, probably more equable and amiable, but
doomed to create images of people round him
rather than to know the living man or woman.
The friends of Lamb about the middle period of
his life were of a remarkable variety; there is no
numbering them, and there were some, at the
India House and elsewhere, of whom we know
nothing but that Lamb's world included them
not less firmly in their way than his pathetic
leader Coleridge of "golden days", his pathetic
follower Martin Burney with the grubby hands
and the spotless character. Lamb ranged in
personal regard and mutuality from Sam Rogers
at his elevated breakfast parties to young Ryle,
the latest recruit at the India House; from the
Guildhall to the greenroom. One cannot readily
conjecture (not forgetting Byron and Shelley, but
they spelt literary forces which Lamb thought
misapplied and perilous), that there was anyone
alive in whom he would fail to discern a
cause for a certain measure of rejoicing at "something that doth live". Let me resort to anecdotes. "I hate Z.", he remarked; and one
standing by said, "Why, you have never seen

him". "No", Lamb agreed: "certainly not, I
never could hate any man that I have once seen."
To someone insisting too much on the depravity
of thieves, Lamb, putting away his pipe, proposed
that a thief was a very good man. To change the
ground, let us recall the timid advent of John
Clare, the Northamptonshire poet, in London,
and at a literary dinner party. Lamb immediately
placed himself by Clare and his snuff-box before
him, and the Peasant was in a short time talking
freely and unreservedly and even opposing his
opinion; the picture suggesting to Thomas Hood
a conference between a House Lamb and a Grass
Lamb. When one such party broke up, Lamb in
his black suit and Clare in his country green
walked behind the others to an exhibition; and
the sight of them thus so delighted an onlooker
or two that there were cries of "There goes
Tom and Jerry". When Clare was once again
in his isolation "among the ignorant like a lost
man", Elia sent him books and such a letter that
it became a family memory. "Friend Lamb",
began Clare, in one of the fine sonnets which
declared his admiration and his affection. Change
the ground a little again—at the same parties
was Thomas Griffiths Wainewright, who was
in later years to be convicted as a forger and
suspected as a poisoner. There grew up round

the name and figure of this fantastic art critic,
from Dickens's day to Wilde's, a rich criminal
legend, shimmering with exotic vice; but that
legend gets no help from any word that Lamb
is known to have written. Wainewright is in
the Letter to Southey as "the light-, and warm-
as light-, hearted Janus of the London [Maga-
zine]", and in the days of Janus's fall Lamb uttered
no recantation. He had met *his* Wainewright.
He had made no mistake. Change the ground
greatly, and see Lamb (who had once been
convinced of Nelson's genuine heroic eminence
by seeing him in the street), confronting Southey
with this view: "After all, Bonaparte is a fine
fellow, as my barber says, and I should not mind
standing bareheaded at his table to do him service in his fall. They should have given him
Hampton Court or Kensington, with a tether
extending forty miles round London. Qu.Would
not the people have ejected the Brunswicks some
day in his favour? Well, we shall see". And
even at this point we must watch our man; for
Lamb, the hearty lampooner of the Brunswick
menagerie, yet informed his friends with a calm
smile, "I love *my* Regent".

These are random suggestions of the sympathies of Lamb in action; but if they produce an
effect of a diffused and indiscriminate philan-

thropy they must fail. For throughout them all there was a distinctness; and Barry Cornwall, who had known many noble characters, looked back through half a century to that fact. "It was curious to observe the gradations in Lamb's manner to his various guests; although it was courteous to all. With Hazlitt he talked as though they met the subject in discussion on equal terms; with Leigh Hunt he exchanged repartees; to Wordsworth he was almost respectful; with Coleridge he was sometimes jocose, sometimes deferring; with Martin Burney fraternally familiar; with Manning affectionate; with Godwin merely courteous; or if friendly, then in a minor degree." Those were only a few of Lamb's friends; let us add a name or two—besides some already given: Haydon the painter, living on loans, panegyrics and futurity; Sheridan Knowles the playwright, Kenney the playwright; Barron Field, the lawyer, critic and student of our older literature; Vincent Novello, the popularizer of great music; William Ayrton, the musical journalist;—there let me break off. To all these men Lamb extended the kind of help that appeared most congenial. For Haydon he wrote and published poems applauding his exhibitions; for Knowles and Kenney he devised prologues and epilogues; to Field he opened his

mind on life and literature, and, when the
younger man went to Australia, Lamb enter-
tained him by letter as though at home, and
reviewed his poems with the frankest cheerful-
ness; Novello's musical labours and joys were
also hailed by Lamb in delightful prose and verse
and even in a review of the publication of "The
Fitzwilliam Music"; Ayrton was cheered with
letters and notably with that sublime rhyming
epistle asking for orders for Mozart's "Don Gio-
vanni". Barry Cornwall himself was welcomed
as a poet in a sonnet of the utmost daintiness and
critical encouragement. Almost every friend of
Lamb held the opinion that he more than anybody else understood Lamb, much as we all have
our invulnerable individual claims of seeing the
true Othello or Timon for the only time in
history. And with all this, the presence of Lamb
at his Wednesday evenings maintained an un-
embarrassed society of persons, well perpetuated
by the really gentle Barry Cornwall, who learned
not to be alarmed when Hazlitt's impetuous
political remarks drove Lamb, sometimes, "into
fierce expressions on public affairs",—and Hazlitt received them in silence. "The beauty of
these evenings was that every one was placed
upon an easy level. No one out-topped the
others. No one—not even Coleridge—was per-

mitted to out-talk the rest. No one was allowed
to hector another, or to bring his own grievances
too prominently forward; so as to disturb the
harmony of the night. Every one had a right to
speak, and to be heard; and no one was ever
trodden or clamoured down (as in some large
assemblies) until he had proved that he was not
entitled to a hearing, or until he had abused his
privilege. I never, in all my life, heard so much
unpretending good sense talked, as at Charles
Lamb's social parties. Often, a piece of sparkling
humour was shot out that illuminated the whole
evening. Sometimes there was a flight of high
and earnest talk, that took one half way toward
the stars."

In his regard for literature and art, Lamb's
sympathies may be traced through sensitive
gradations too; for he has ways of revelation beyond ordinary tallies of approval or adoration.
A quotation of his, a phrase borrowed and new-
grown into his prose, may tell us much. He may
be proved an old friend of such a non-Elizabethan
poet as Young, of the "Night Thoughts", by a
witty recollection of a fine verse; but he does not
write of Young at all—his bellman is Webster,
and of him we have remembered Lamb's vision.
He celebrates "books with one idea in them", as
the "Pilgrim" of Bishop Patrick, sometimes

dragged into daylight on account of a supposed consanguinity with Bunyan's "Pilgrim"; "the freezing, appalling, petrifying dullness of that book", he concludes, "is quite astounding. Yet there is one lively image in the preface...." He obeys the advice of Pope so far as to peruse Charron on Wisdom, says he was "betrayed", but comes away grateful for one "piece of gorgeous and happy eloquence". Pope, on the evidence of many allusions and shadowings, would be one of his genuine if not giant authors; but he spent time and money in bringing home to his fold the ragged productions of the victims of "The Dunciad". Donne and Cowley, to his judgment, had a "warmth of soul and generous feeling" which "forty thousand" of such poets praised for naturalness as Shenstone "with all their quantity, could not make up"; yet he writes of "the dear author of 'The School-mistress'". He affects to scorn the romantic wildness of Germany, and invents the preposterous rhyme,

> Goëthe, Goëthe,
> What a beauty;

and when Abraham Hayward's translation of "Faust", satisfactory to a generation, appears presently, it is the writer's pride to point out that his work was primarily due to a remark of Charles Lamb's. Everybody has a notion of the books which Lamb, or Elia—for I am here free of chronological limits—described as unreadable: books which "no gentleman's library should be without"; but where do we find men like him who have read not only Sir Thomas More's "Utopia" but also "a massive folio of his Theological Works in English, partly Practical Divinity, but for the greater part Polemic, against the grand Lutheran Heresy"? He could invade such realms of Chaos and Old Night, because, as he enjoined upon his reader, he realized the art of "putting himself into the feelings of an auditory of More's Creed and Times". The name "More" gives me another move; another folio that Lamb possessed (and one of a tribe) was Dr Henry More's "Collection of Several Philosophical Writings", some of which angered him. Against More's vivisectional statement, "I having seen with mine own eyes a frog quite exenterated, heart, stomach, guts, and all taken out by an ingenious friend of mine, and dexterous anatomist; after which the frog would see, and avoid any object in its way", the bookman wrote, "He would avoid you and your damned friend, and have no very great brain in his guts neither". None the less

Lamb esteemed his Henry More, and copied gladly into the book such passages by him and about him as should do him honour; thus, "Dr More after finishing some of his writings, 'Now for these three months I will neither think a wise thought, nor speak a wise word, nor do an ill thing'". And Lamb had read not only his Henry More, but the biographer of that Platonist with perfect attention.

What had he not read? The catalogue of his library, apart from his sheer reading, cannot now be ascertained completely. It is a rich study in thoughtfulness to scan even the limited series of titles preserved by his biographers. Who besides Lamb and the improvisers of theses *en route* for academic diplomas has ever made MS. notes and additions to the publications of John Dennis, ridiculed by Pope's set? or passed from them to Donne (we are very proud of discovering Donne) and shared the margins with Coleridge in "curious and valuable critical and illustrative notes"; or from Donne to Drayton ("the blank leaves are crowded with illustrative extracts from Elizabethan authors, additional poems, &c. including the whole of Skelton's 'Philip Sparrow' in Lamb's hand"—we admire ourselves for discovering Skelton); or from Drayton to Drummond (in America with the others); or thence

to John Dryden? The essays of Lamb may not
exhibit his opinion of Dryden but it has been
recorded by his friend, and pupil in prose writing,
P. G. Patmore (who had a son); "Lamb spoke
of Dryden as a prodigious person, so far as his
wonderful power of versification went, but not
a first-rate poet, or even capable of appreciating
such—giving instances from his prefaces in proof
of this. He spoke of Dryden's prefaces as the
finest pieces of *criticism*, nevertheless, that had
ever been written, and the better for being con-
tradictory to each other, because not founded on
any pretended *rules*". Homage to John Dryden!

CHAPTER VI

ELIA

If it is the definition of a book to be the sustained product of a well-conceived design, the foreseen result of an idea and accumulated materials, then the annoying author whose advance into middle age I have traced never wrote a book. We know the manner in which he was accustomed to refer to the two volumes called his "Works", published in 1818, pointing out that these were his recreations, and that his true works were the hundred folios or so which he had filled up in the service of the East India Company. What is more, he showed a sturdy reluctance to produce any books, by the regular standard. It was in vain that Wordsworth, perceiving his power of characterization and of atmosphere, urged him to write a novel. Lamb remained an author "by turns, and nothing long"; and this fact had nothing to do with his powers of mind and of invention, which we see as well as if they had formed us a set of volumes as numerous as Goethe's. Rather, it was his essential decision or criticism that restrained him; he had not the conditions of life in which he might envisage a great construction of the imaginative faculty, therefore he kept away from any harassed and uncertain attempt. Lamb's reverence for the highest literature is expressed in this as much as in any of his tributes to genius ancient and modern. And yet, he was destined to create what has been counted for over a century one of the best books—one, which almost every new adventure in the republication of classics includes very early in the list. The latest edition of "Elia" is a sumptuous one from the most noble, perhaps, of the semi-private presses in the kingdom, and is already—"out of print"; but there will be many more. I cannot think of any other single collection of prose papers since 1823 which has had quite such a history of unfailing audiences. Macaulay is a worthy monument, and full of information and opinion; names like Pater, like Stevenson, like Edmund Gosse are not bloomless yet; some of our contemporaries have held their place for a decade or two,—it is twelve years since Mr Aldous Huxley was Autolycus of the *Athenaeum*; and I must not forget our chieftain Mr Birrell of "Obiter Dicta", and wish for more of the same. But when finally one reflects on the essayists who exist in their books without noticeable decline, and are not confined to any particular cabal or interest or need of the race of readers, the catalogue becomes a brief one from Montaigne to Bacon, and from Bacon to Lamb.

But still, if on this consideration Lamb did write a book, he stumbled into it without ambition; no preliminary operation orders were circulated through the coteries and the columns; he gave himself none. It is well to recall exactly the title under which, when enough papers were ready to be brought out together, Lamb published: "Elia: Essays which have appeared under that Signature in the London Magazine". The invention which was the nearest element in this to the deliberate framing of a masterpiece was simply Elia, a phantom personality; and for this invention Lamb was eager to disclaim any strong quality of authorship. He was for laughing it off; others might interpret;—one read the name as the anagram for "a lie", another was for making the public know that Elia merely meant Lamb; but Lamb was against any anagrams and identifications. It was a name that he had borrowed from an old fellow clerk, to avoid giving offence to his brother John; another time it was a name without any meaning. The

curiosity aroused by his device or mask gave
him small pleasure when it appeared in print;
he "answered a fool according to his folly" with
malicious, or rather with pugnacious fabrications
of a family of Elias that had flourished formerly
in "stately Genoa". He could not easily bear
to have his essay-character fixed like a pair of
shafts to his sides: his motto was perhaps, "I
cannot pull a cart or eat dried oats". To have a
square formula fixed upon one's name is one of
the rewards and penalties of all who delight their
fellow-men with one kind of writing once; and
Lamb was, vainly enough I suppose, endeavouring
in the day of his success to dodge this localization.

But I am straying ahead of the theme which
is properly due here: the plain history of these
essays, as they came into the world. It is a
history which comprises a distinctly melancholy
side-show, for those who can feel in an age like
ours, with plenty to darken our vision, any re-
grets about the literary scene of a century since.
I mean the splendid failure of Taylor and Hessey's
London Magazine, and perhaps with that goes
the equally splendid failure of Taylor and
Hessey as publishers. In that partnership, John
Taylor was the principal. He possessed several
intellectual gifts, from a skill in questions of
currency and economics to that of recognizing

and analysing the poetry of such men as John
Keats and John Clare. Indeed, he perceived
almost without mistake who were the men of
genius, as distinct from the temporary heroes, of
his time. In this way he became the publisher of
Keats, Lamb, Clare, Hazlitt, Landor, H. F. Cary,
George Darley, Coleridge (his "Aids to Reflection"), De Quincey and others not unworthy
of these names, and within a few years had
achieved a remarkable position in the chronicles
of that seldom sufficiently honoured race the
publishers. But Taylor was an unsuccessful
judge of men. Probably too great confidence
in his own abilities prevented him from giving
the eminent minds whom he had gathered about
him the liberty of action which they needed.
He alienated them too soon by his precise,
cautious, corrective and obstinate methods,
whether it was Landor the inflammable or Clare
the sensitive. Besides that, the firm of Taylor
and Hessey, publishing such beautiful creations
as "Endymion" and "Elia" and hardly anything that did not claim a place in the history of
sound literature, met with the difficulties of such
eclectic trade. The partners went their ways, and
the work that they had done remained a single
storey of the pyramid, no more.

Of the *London Magazine*, the most valuable

literary periodical while it flourished that has
ever appeared in this country, the same may
be said. It was originally under the editorship
of John Scott, whose powerful double gifts of
obtaining the best from other writers and of
showing them the example of astute and eloquent
writing of his own instantly distinguished it. On
one side he could gain the services of Elia, on
the other he could write such a complete and
timely critical study as that of Keats. That name
involves a calamity here; for out of a dispute
with *Blackwood's* relating to the abuse of the
young poet outpoured from that camp, it came
about that Scott's career was ended in a duel in
February 1821. And this pitiable sacrifice must
have the additional discord in it that Keats did
not like John Scott. Within a few months the
London was taken over from the proprietors
by Taylor and Hessey. There was some talk of
Hazlitt's being appointed editor, and Thomas
Hood was employed as a subordinate, but the
earnest literary habit of Taylor induced him to
proceed without any other editorship than what
he—and he was a tough worker, an indefatigable
corrector and adviser—could give to it among
his other preoccupations. From 1821 to the end
of 1823 this loose arrangement worked remarkably well within its limits, and the *London* was

alike a present wealth and a great hope; if
aridity and dogma reigned in some contemporaries, here was an oasis,

A place of nestling green for fine souls made.

Such series of articles as Hazlitt's "Table-Talk",
De Quincey's "Opium Eater" and that which I
am especially reconsidering were by no means
isolated in their spirit of free thought and dream,
but were harmonious with a profusion of good
prose and poetry from many friends who met at
Waterloo Place to dine together as the "Londoners." There was for a time a cordial interplay
of all the talents. But Taylor's besetting vanity
and his understandable exhaustion led to the
decline of this promising morning sunshine in
that world of journalism; and then appeared the
regrettable but fairly well attested fact that a
magazine may be too good, to use the ordinary
phrase, to obtain a necessary circulation. The
remedy that was handiest was to raise the price,
but that depressed the public. In 1825 there was
little doubt that the spirit of the *London Magazine* had chiefly evaporated, as the dinners of
the contributors had vanished; and Taylor and
Hessey resigned their former favourite into hands
which never looked like preserving the little life
that was still in it—with which obituary notice

may be associated the dissolution no very long time afterwards of the partnership, so unusually distinguished in the authors it had gained and stimulated.

The short spell of reputation which this *Magazine* enjoyed was due principally to Elia, as even the satirical Tom Moore noted; yet let me spy out the situation through a contemporary glass —the *Edinburgh Review*, which indicates a further reason why the *Magazine* did not endure. "Which is the best, the London, or the New Monthly? We are not the Oedipus to solve this riddle; and indeed it might be difficult, for we believe many of the writers are the same in each. But both contain articles, in the form of Essays, Theatrical Criticism, *Jeux-d'-Esprit*, which may be considered as the flower and cream of periodical literature....Are there not the quaint and grave subtleties of Elia, the extreme paradoxes of the author of Table-talk, the Confessions of an Opium-eater, the copious tales of Traditional Literature, all from one Magazine?..." The notice alludes to the "sustained tone of general reflection, of mild sentiment and liberal taste" there, as representative of the age; and continues, "The fault of the London Magazine is, that it wants a sufficient unity of direction and purpose. There is no particular bias or governing spirit,—which neutralizes the interest. The articles seem thrown into the letter-box, and to come up like blanks and prizes in the lottery— all is in a confused, unconcocted state, like the materials of a rich plum-pudding before it has been well boiled".

That fault was none of Lamb's, who was honoured both within the intimate circle of the *Magazine* and beyond. Taylor and Hessey paid him at a much higher rate than their other contributors, which is no mean form of critical respect. The Essays, as they appeared, were quoted and even transplanted into other periodicals; the "New Year's Eve", for instance, became instantly a special offering of the *Morning Chronicle* to its readers. As the author of Elia, the clerk of the India House was invited to a dinner at the Mansion House,—"and all", he mischievously remarked, "from being a writer in a magazine". And incidentally this writer did not miss the tribute of being abused and ridiculed by a few reviewers. To turn to simple record, Lamb sent Elia forth with the *London Magazine* in August 1820, the first essay being the "Recollections of the South Sea House"; in October came "Oxford in the Vacation", in November "Christ's Hospital Five and Thirty Years Ago", and the following month "The

Two Races of Men". This was a generous succession of originalities, quite startling over the
signature of one Elia; a new prose writer, to
many readers, had arisen from the common level
of wit and social observation, a subtler, more
tuneable, more friendly and yet more remote personality than they had known yet. The four
unforgettable essays mentioned were only the
firstfruits; throughout 1821 and 1822 the harvest
was pretty well continual, and at the end of 1822
the first of the two "Elia" volumes was issued.
The separate publication was hardly sent out to
friends before Lamb produced in the *Magazine*
his "Character of the late Elia", by way of
suggesting that the half-assumed personality had
now been accorded a sufficient hearing, and that
he would not keep him in the world any longer.
And yet in the same number of the *Magazine*
Elia's Ghost was permitted to lead the "Re-
joicings on the New Year's Coming of Age".
In short, the impersonation was not allowed to
be dropped so soon; Lamb had become a kind of
institution as Elia, and from time to time Elia
embodied his moods and meditations afresh as
delightfully as before. "Old China" in the *London* for March 1823 was an infallible proof that
the phantom was not to be forced to vanish so
suddenly; in spite of Lamb's studied indirection,

a direction had been forced upon him; and even
when writing for other magazines in another
degree of make-believe, at later dates, Lamb was
liable to sign himself[1] still "Elia". It was not
until 1833 that "The Last Essays of Elia. Being
a Sequel to Essays published under that Name"
were gathered into one of Moxon's typo-
graphically flawless volumes; but the sense of
any gulf of time or of idea between the first and
second series has long fallen into disuse; one
cannot think now of any tolerable edition which
should not contain the two together. As one
work, I shall now approach them from the point
of view of critical estimation.

The essay, as a type of writing, was not un-
examined in its development by Lamb, though
he had no ambitions in the field of a Saintsbury
or a "Cambridge History". He read his Montaigne in Florio's or Cotton's translation. He
rebelled against that line of Pope's of "sage
Montaigne, or more sage Charron", retorting:
"Montaigne is an immense treasure-house of
observation, anticipating all the discoveries of
succeeding essayists. You cannot dip in him without being struck with the aphorism, that there is

[1] Or to allow the signature to appear. "Ex-Elia",
he subscribes to one of his letters, and in another
tells Moxon to omit "the sickening Elia".

nothing new under the sun. All the writers on
common life since him have done nothing but
echo him. You cannot open him without de-
tecting a Spectator, or starting a Rambler; besides that his own character pervades the whole,
and binds it sweetly together". Allusions in his
works show that Lamb was a good judge of
Bacon's formal wisdom in column-of-fours; we
met him as a child in a window-seat with Cowley's book in his lap; and one of the passages that
Mr Tillyard marks out as among his beautiful
adjustments in literary appreciation is that called
"The Genteel Style in Writing", a study of
Sir William Temple in his essays. The reser-
vation that Lamb mainly makes in praising
Temple brings us from the seventeenth century
to the eighteenth: "On one occasion his wit,
which was mostly subordinate to nature and
tenderness, has seduced him into a string of
felicitous antitheses; which, it is obvious to remark, have been a model to Addison and succeeding essayists". Lamb's condemnations are
rarely sweeping, and this one is only partial;
for his pages declare him a faithful reader of
the *Tatler* and the *Spectator*, a friend of Isaac
Bickerstaff and Will Honeycomb. He has written
of the "undying midnight lamp" of Bickerstaff
—a noble praise, but carefully chosen. The habit

of browsing among neglected and rejected books took Lamb now and then into the region of less famous eighteenth-century periodical essayists than Addison and Steele—the innumerable host of them from Babbler to Lounger, from Mist's Miscellany Letters to Dennis's Original Letters, Familiar, Moral and Critical. The sum of these observations is that when Lamb began to practise the art of the essay, in spite of the geniality of several of the recent practitioners, he found the form subject to a heavy convention. It was a public oration, for the most part, whether humorous or serious; its studies of characters were, for all their solidity of observation, only stage exhibitions; its arguments were those of the platform or the chairman's place, excellent in their way but constructed by intellectual brick-laying; its chief "day out" took the form of an allegorical vision, in which angels meant further arguments of strictly moral value, one at a time. From all this machinery, which had served the coffee-house and the country house very credit-ably from the days of Steele to those of the popular essayist whom Lamb ventured to call "stupid Knox" (he flourished at the close of the 18th century), it seemed time to release the genius of personal talk and give it wings again. Montaigne had lived long enough ago.

But, it may be objected, had not Goldsmith imparted freshness and happiness to the port-stained essay, forty years before Lamb tried his hand? May I suffer for it if I do injustice now or ever to that elder ghost of the Temple and of Islington. Let Goldsmith's introductory essay speak for him of his attitude towards the function of an essayist; we remember how, when his bookseller was suggesting to him a "promising plan to smooth up our readers a little", the essayist "thought proper to decline, by assuring him, that as I intended to pursue no fixed method, so it was impossible to form any regular plan: determined never to be tedious in order to be logical; wherever pleasure presented, I was re-solved to follow". Let me find in Goldsmith a sentence or so which perhaps could be mistaken for one of Lamb's artful intimations: in that page where he amuses us with his two Quack Doctors. "And yet the great have their foibles as well as the little. I am almost ashamed to mention it. Let the foibles of the great rest in peace. Yet I must impart the whole. These two great men are actually now at variance; like mere men, mere common mortals.—Rock advises the world to beware of bog-trotting quacks: Frank retorts the wit and the sarcasm, by fixing on his rival the odious appellation of Dumpling Dick. He

calls the serious doctor Rock, Dumpling Dick!
Head of Confucius, what profanation!" True,
there is an Elianish whim about this—a rudi-
mentary fantastical philanthropy. But even Goldsmith's essays incline to be moral provision-
stores, whence you may take home good honest
sober parcels of reflection and anecdote for
domestic use.

When it is admitted that from all the essayists
named and hinted, who were accessible reading
down to the years of "Elia", Lamb naturally
derived some method and tone; when it is added
that—for instance—the eighteenth-century table-
talker Shenstone probably gave the notion of
the "Detached Thoughts on Books and Reading",
and that Lamb surely took up the very title
from Cooke's popular edition of Shenstone,[1]—
still, his achievement of a new sort of egotism by

[1] In it you find Detached Thoughts on Publications,
on Books &c., on Writing and Books, on Books and
Writers, on Men and Manners. Here is a word from
Shenstone: "The writer who gives us the best idea
of what may be called the genteel in style and manner
of writing, is, in my opinion, my Lord Shaftesbury".
Elia (notwithstanding his severer definition of
Shaftesbury in "The Genteel Style in Writing",
1826): "I have no repugnances. Shaftesbury is not
too genteel for me, nor Jonathan Wild too low".

way of essay stands out clear; and the question remains, how he performed this beautiful process of liberation and enrichment? from what sympathies and recognitions? One part of the answer is, the inheritance and training of Lamb. He was blessed with the power of seeing life actually and in vision too; was unconfined, and would not confine; was various, and worshipped infinite variety. In him contested sadness and frolic, the weary weight of things and the exhilaration of spiritual intuitions; endless was the delicate or dramatic variation as these elements interacted in him. From such a nervous temperament, and inward paradox, it would have been strange had conventional writings been the outward result, and above all where the object of his taking pen in hand was to confess himself. Lamb in the body once sat in the stocks at Barnet, but he was not to be clapped into any metaphysical frame of wood when he was speaking of his adventures and dreams as truly as he could recall them. This, I believe, is the first half of an explanation of his "Elia", transforming the general conception of an essay's range, depth, and coruscation. The other half verges towards the technical. Whence did he piece out his theory and practice of prose writing, as "Elia" reveals them? The answer here would be, from any

ELIA

authors almost except formal essayists. He perceived that the course of his predecessors had gradually become a sunk road, whence you could not see the landscape or receive the open sun and wind; he changed all that.

> Not from essay-writers only,
> When essays come, breaks in the light.

To take an instance: he had his "Tristram Shandy", his "Sentimental Journey", in which the force of sudden silences, of the broken sentence and fine phrase lingering as though (and it was no contrivance) there were no words to add just then. Here he learned, so far as he needed to be taught, the significant brevity, the quiet but abrupt resumption in another voice. From his older authors—most of all, I take it, from the "beautiful obliquities" of Sir Thomas Browne—Lamb inhaled the sweet science of a rich and labyrinthine prose, into which he proceeds on occasions of "a solemn music", and which combining with the laconic style mentioned creates an excitement and a triumph of expression. In the first essay of Elia,[1] you have both of Lamb's imaginative movements of prose. He gives us his symphony of a reverie: "This was once a house of trade,—a centre of busy

[1] In the *London* for 1820.

interests. The throng of merchants was here—
the quick pulse of gain—and here some forms
of business are still kept up, though the soul be
long since fled. Here are still to be seen stately
porticos; imposing staircases; offices roomy as
the state apartments in palaces—deserted, or
thinly peopled with a few straggling clerks; the
still more sacred interiors of court and com-
mittee rooms, with venerable faces of beadles,
door-keepers—directors seated in form on solemn
days (to proclaim a dead dividend), at long
worm-eaten tables, that have been mahogany,
with tarnished gilt-leather coverings, supporting
massy silver inkstands long since dry;—the
oaken wainscots hung with pictures of deceased
governors and sub-governors, of Queen Anne,
and the two first monarchs of the Brunswick dynasty;—huge charts, which subsequent
discoveries have antiquated;—dusty maps of
Mexico, dim as dreams,—and soundings of the
Bay of Panama!—The long passages hung with
buckets, appended in idle rows, to walls whose
substance might defy any, short of the last,
conflagration:—with vast ranges of cellarage
under all, where dollars and pieces of eight once
lay, an 'unsunned heap', for Mammon to have
solaced his solitary heart withal,—long since
dissipated, or scattered into air at the blast of

the breaking of that famous BUBBLE.—'' With
this to haunt the mind in its livelong fullness,
Lamb turns to the human faces and voices that
he knew, "passing away", in the ghost-like
House; and then at last, he will puzzle us with
another manner: "Reader, what if I have been
playing with thee all this while—peradventure
the very *names*, which I have summoned up
before thee, are fantastic—insubstantial—like
Henry Pimpernel and old John Naps of Greece:—
Be satisfied that something answering to them
has had a being. Their importance is from the
past". But, in truth, his feeling for the impres-
sive changes of length and stress in sentence and
paragraph is everywhere exquisite and pro-
ductive. It is through this accomplishment that
parodists of Elia, having hit off something like his
phrase, have failed to suggest his individuality.

From Browne, from Fuller, from Jeremy
Taylor and Burton he drew, not the pleasure he
had and gives in the unexpected and eccentric
phrase, but the confidence in such ingeniousness.
He did not revive their loved conceits without
rebuke, and the rebuke came amongst others
from the drastic Hazlitt. At their best, Lamb's
recurrences to the old fantastic way are, to many
tastes at any rate, wonderfully eloquent. When
he will have us receive in an instant the virtues

of Roast Pig, he does it thus: "Of all the delicacies in the whole *mundus edibilis*, I will maintain it to be the most delicate—*princeps obsonio-
rum*", and even if our Latinity is defeated our
minds are seized with the lordly flourish. When
he tells an anecdote of Elliston at supper, who
only took one dish—"reckoning fish as nothing",
he would have us appreciate it highly; "The
manner", he adds, "was all. It was as if by one
peremptory sentence he had decreed the anni-
hilation of all the savoury esculents, which the
pleasant and nutritious-food-giving Ocean pours
forth upon poor humans from her watery bosom".
The Homeric parody here seems the only way
in which Elliston's grandeur might be shadowed
forth. But shorter phrases equally show Lamb's
command of the language of wit-melancholy,
whether he is referring to the people of Hastings
as "unsophisticated aborigines", to small jests
as "twinkling corpuscula", to young sweeps as
"tender novices, blooming through their first
nigritude", or to the departed actor manager
"in Green Rooms, impervious to mortal eye,
wielding posthumous empire". Lamb has himself made his reply to those who objected to
Elia's "affected array of antique modes and
phrases. They had not been *his*, if they had been
other than such; and better it is, that a writer

should be natural in a self-pleasing quaintness, than to affect a naturalness (so called) that should be strange to him". And yet surely he has insisted on his archaisms too often; the audacious curiosity of circumlocutions has its own special work and attraction, but too many "peradventures", "haths", "wouldst thous" seem to clog the attention.

There is one of Lamb's minor arts in his essays which may have been implanted in him by the "Anatomy of Melancholy", if by any book: it is his expertness of quotation, and mis-quotation, and parodic recollection. Possibly on this very merit of his he has been dismissed in modern times as "just literary", but the same times have applauded the poets Mr Eliot and Dr Bridges for their gift of weaving into their own verse the radiant phrase of former genius, and I do not think that there is a general case against Lamb for anticipating them with this associative method. On the contrary, he seems to me to play on the writings of others with almost perfect touch, now whimsical, now serious in conjuring up some other spirit than his to join his theme. It may take us all our time to catch what precisely he is at, but the delay is worth while. Thus, where he complains cheerfully of Coleridge's ruinous borrowings of odd volumes,

he says, "In yonder nook, John Buncle, a
widower-volume, with 'eyes closed', mourns his
ravished mate". The "ravished mate" part of it
is an irreverent echo of a passage in Thomson's
"Seasons", of which the pathos has worn thin;
if you look to a commentator on Elia, you are
informed correctly that the "eyes closed" is a
quotation from the book of Buncle, who mourned
his wives that way. But the quotation is a double
one; for (I hope I am not astray) Lamb is
laughing at Coleridge in a just sufficient re-
miniscence of "Kubla Khan", S. T. C.'s own:

> Weave a circle round him thrice,
> And close your eyes with holy dread.

Where a work is so firmly established as to
suffer nothing from a sly pleasant misuse, there
is Lamb, ready to add a quality to his own good-
humoured presence in prose: in his "Quaker's
Meeting" he abbreviates the solemn Abbey scene
of Congreve's "Mourning Bride" in order to
convey the silent spectacle,

> How reverend is the view of these hushed heads,
> Looking tranquillity;

all statuary comes into the impression; and a few
moments afterwards he pokes a little fun at
Wordsworth's pretty rhymes as he describes the

unanimity of the Meeting—"Their garb and stillness conjoined present an uniformity, tranquil and herd-like—as in the pasture—'forty feeding like one'". Lamb's quotations, as I believe St Paul's were, are usually of an application not intended by the authors. But they do not lose caste in the process. For some less familiar poets he has contrived a touch of immortality. Whatever the destructive power of Marvell and Dryden over the name of Flecknoe, Lamb has seen to it that Flecknoe is at that same Quaker's Meeting, in an inspired prayer to Silence. For some less familiar poems by authors of renown, Lamb does the same; who but he would have shown that Pope's uneasy "Ode on Saint Cecilia's Day" was not all fustian, as he does in repeating the lines,

> Or under hanging mountains,
> Or by the fall of fountains?

He, I fancy, is really the poet at such times, giving the words of others a new import, a new emotion. Sometimes Lamb quotes straight out, in deep emotion; perhaps there has never been a more powerful and saddening change of mood than one in the "Chimney-Sweepers" essay, when, having been celebrating as though it was immediately and vociferously present the feast that he and his friend gave the climbing-boys, he stops, and utters Shakespeare's words,

> Golden lads and lasses must,
> As chimney-sweepers, come to dust.

"JAMES WHITE" (he goes on) "is extinct, and with him these suppers have long ceased."

I shall now, too briefly, glance at the Essays of Elia, familiar as they are, with an eye to one or two of their broad achievements. Altogether they correspond to that tag of "a little volume but great book". They are not very numerous, but they include a surprising variety of subject, of experience, of treatment; in subject, they range from the vision of beautiful children that never were to be to the drollery consequent upon old George Dyer's tumbling into the New River's tenuous trickle, from nonsensical rebellion against Beethoven, Bach, Mozart to the contemplation of true and false imaginative painting. Their autobiographical animation is sustained from the child Elia's small and magic world of the Temple sundials and fountains to the man's superannuation from his daily work of year on year, and his sense of a "dark companionship" already beckoning him away from his dear earth. We share over and over again a beauty of incident and encounter like that pretty difficulty Lamb

had as he sat on Primrose Hill reading "Pamela"
and a "familiar damsel" insisted on reading
ahead with him; we live with Elia in dreams,
traversing those distinct "cities abroad, which
I have never seen, and hardly have hope to see",
—in his speculations too, "Sun and sky, and
breeze, and solitary walks, and summer holidays,
and the greenness of fields, and the delicious
juices of meats and fishes, and society, and the
cheerful glass, and fire-side conversations, and
innocent vanities, and jests, and *irony* itself—do
these things go out with life?" In treatment,
almost every essay moves through a series of
modes; wild and sweet, grave and subdued, clear
and practical, sumptuous and sonorous—Elia is
all these. I must remember Lamb's warning
that "we must be modest for a modest man",
but the panegyrical afflatus is not the source of
these terms. They are promiscuous, meagre and
fragmentary, the Essays are differenced, many-
blossomed and handsome.

From them, as though from a series of novels
—and it is hard that Lamb did not for once act on
Wordsworth's advice—a number of spirits or
figures have found their way into the hearts of
the English and American reading worlds[1]. Elia
himself—not Lamb precisely, but dressed very

[1] I should add especially, the Japanese too.

much like Lamb in black, with "immaterial legs" tidily gaitered—is not allowed to die; he stoops along past every file of London schoolchildren, fearing to "be taken for a governor", and is in every old college library, smiling at the marshalled erudition of this queer race. Bridget Elia still ties her bonnet as she crosses the stiles towards—any farmhouse in Hertfordshire, and Mrs Battle has refused to take up bridge, and sits with her book recalling "a clear fire, a clean hearth and the rigour of the game" before these developments. That careful classical scholar George Dyer and his works are dust; but Lamb's G. D. is still tolerably well, and represents the absent-minded devotee of what he never will understand more famously than does the lifelike portrait of Dyer—and his enchanted dog Daphne—that hangs in the Fitzwilliam Museum. Boyer, the shark-like infester—as some would say—of the backwaters of old Christ's Hospital, holds on his way, and in Elia's wide vision murmurs mildly to us now. Milder Susan P—— is comforted for ever for the sometime death of Samuel Salt, who is not lost, but there in the essay with her. Joseph Munden, the comedian, is protected from the nemesis of actors; he still "stands wondering" on the stage, creating abstracts out of chairs and pint pots, "amid the commonplace materials of life, like primeval man with the sun and stars about him". Captain Jackson and his daughters genteelize still in their cottage on the Bath road, and plated spoons of theirs become silver sugar tongs, and a poor spinet yields celestial, Cecilian melodies. These and other friends to man are the legacy of Elia; or part of it, for he has invested his whole world, buildings, streets, fields, with happy auguries, at once encouraging his readers to a closer and finer relation with their fellow-men, and the gifts of the gods, and to a peculiar confidence in what is to be. But Lamb would counter this in an instant with his declaration—let science dwell on it as a motto for the next assaults on Time—that he wrote for Antiquity.

CHAPTER VII

ELIA'S FAREWELL

The last decade of Lamb's life—from 1824 to
1834—is not the only end to a life that echoes
Blake's saying, "Nature has no tune". The
principal incident in it affecting his daily habits
was his leaving the India House, after 35 years'
service, on March 29th, 1825, and becoming
a pensioner; what he made of that change will be
a theme in these concluding reflections, but I
do not think he made a tune of his emancipation,
and in general his later experiences echo un-
certainly through the records we have of them.
Nor was this only his case; the period found his
coevals "going or gone", though their superannuated state was variously veiled by reputation
and activity. Towards the end of 1835 Wordsworth, surviving without complete decline, was
to write the elegy on the series of poets who
had departed—on James Hogg, and Scott, and
Coleridge, and Lamb, and Crabbe, and one to
whom we have all owed a tender romantic

moment in our time—Mrs Hemans. Not all the
former visionaries, of course, had departed;
Robert Southey was still wrestling for a long-
endurance trophy, a mighty good-conduct prize.
Leigh Hunt was writing as flexibly and as pro-
spectively as ever, and indeed had it in him still
to challenge his younger self with essays, plays,
poems and finally a noble "Autobiography"—
yet he had been more like a genius when he
edited *The Examiner* and published "Rimini"
amid mingled bouquets and exasperation. Hazlitt,
who could not be in Wordsworth's poem, had
vanished,—a hero in slippers, denied to the end
the clear course which should have been granted
one so wise in his very confusions.

It was not only in the passing of a great
literary generation that the years of which I
speak were uneasy ones to live through; so far
as literary taste in England was concerned, they
involved an obscurity and an artificiality which
to men like Lamb was unwelcome. This may
be fairly illustrated by the mention of the
Annuals which came into fashion now—the "For-
get-Me-Not", the "Keepsake", "Literary Sou-
venir", "Amulet", "Friendship's Offering" and
any number more,—the exquisite registers, perhaps, of more money than sense. They gained a
very great popularity as representative selections,

and those artists and authors who had not the
luck, the knack, or the wish to contribute to them
were accordingly at a disadvantage; for while
these occupied the publishers and the readers so
intently, the chances of quiet good verse and
prose, both as to its being published and to its
being read, were greatly decreased. Moreover,
contributing to them implied a surrender to
fashionable patterns,—to the Byronic tradition
or to that of Miss Landon. This subject is not
instanced here without Lamb's support, for he
suffered in his turn from the Annuals, finally
recoiling from the vain attempt to be one of this
literary assembly. Meanwhile, a state of affairs
was produced in which such a poet as Hood could
send forth a volume of fine fancy, music and
emotion without attracting any real attention;
or, to give another example, John Clare, whose
rougher "Poems Descriptive of Rural Life and
Scenery" had been the critics' and the common
readers' pleasure in 1820, was reduced in 1832
to trying to issue his new collection (far and
away superior to the first) by subscription. That
failed. The less resolute minds in imaginative
literature, the Darleys and the Hartley Cole-
ridges, were repressed and damaged by the
apathy which had succeeded the triumphs of
Byron, Scott, Crabbe and Moore; and it must

have been difficult to avoid an impression that
for all the march of mind and refinement of
manners the country had exchanged a sound
and an eager taste for a false one. Would the
new world have profited much after all by the
energies of such as Wordsworth, and Coleridge,
and Lamb—whose "Elia", be it remembered,
well as it made him known, reached no second
edition in England until after his death? Literary
the land had certainly become, to the extent that
it received and replaced at its circulating libraries
an endless series of printed amusements; but the
"rigour of the game" was threatened.

For Charles Lamb as an author, the years after
the original collection of "Elia" were not
particularly fertile. Being let loose from the
India House might have seemed likely to give
him impulse and sustained leisure for what, as I
have said, even "Elia" was not—a fully planned
work. Doubtless he had in his time seen too
much of Coleridge's mighty dream-children
quarto and octavo to feel a passion for converting his own inveterate occasional way into a
large design,—to join the captains of this industry, and march through innumerable blank
sheets for Colburn or Murray. Must we suppose
that Lamb in view of his endowments never could
have written for us a novel of the scale of

"Tristram Shandy", or a critical study comparable with "Biographia Literaria", or a collection of Poems Chiefly Autobiographical in steady evolution? It has been my task in part to point out that—apart from his conditions of life and his exhausting loyalties—he revealed the possession of powers equal to anyone's of his time; had been, in some lights, the most remarkable of the young poets and critics of the 1790's, and with a few swift strokes in early manhood had stated a new critical guidance and glory. But he was to remain an incidental creator of literature to the end, having stayed too long, it may be, with

"Improbus labor" which my spirits hath broke,

to renew the springs of imaginative abundance and delight. It perhaps seemed to him, towards the close, that he had been a failure in the art of literature; twice he wrote down some account of his authorship for friendly eyes, and the last time was just before his death, when, with a tired and irregular hand, he scribbled an elegiac adieu to numberless articles in prose and verse scattered about the periodicals and irrecoverably lost.[1] I fancy that such references, modest as they were,

[1] This document is in America; I do not know that it has appeared except in facsimile in a sale catalogue.

had the effect of consoling him a little for the
sense he had of his having missed the highroad
of his early mind. And it is apparent that he
liked to think of the service he had done to the
Elizabethan dramatists, by his unanticipated and
permanent anthology—a substantial work, not
an occasional feat.

Aware as he was that the old drama had not
been worked out for its poetical excellences by
that wide study and selection, and feeling that his
new allowance of time ought not to be wasted,
Lamb in 1826 resumed his readings and tran-
scriptions at the British Museum. "I am going
through a course of reading at the Museum: the
Garrick plays, out of part of which I formed my
Specimens: I have Two Thousand to go thro';
and in a few weeks have despatched the tythe
of them. It is a sort of Office to me; hours,
10 to 4, the same. It does me good. Man must
have regular occupation, that has been used to
it." Yet he was not now able to attack his subject with the inspiration which had formerly
spoken such truths of critical insight for the first
time. He says, it is true, that since 1807 he had
discovered the Garrick collection to be "a
treasure rich and exhaustless beyond what I then
imagined", he confesses his luxury of sitting in
old Montagu House "culling at will the flower"

of the mighty England of Beaumont and Fletcher.
Nevertheless, he did not bring away with him a
comparable wealth. "By those who remember
the 'Specimens', these must be considered as
mere after-gleanings, supplementary to that
work, only comprising a longer period. You
must be content with sometimes a scene, sometimes a song; a speech or passage, or a poetical
image, as they happen to strike me." His notes
now, though choice and innovative, had not the
effect of instantly rolling away the ruins of time
from the treasure that the earlier ones had; they
were rather *marginalia* than *principia*. Of Webster, for instance, he had formerly transported a
considerable element into a passage of high command in itself; to that audacious original he had
made his daring answer, which would compel
the listener to summon up all his own comprehension and adore the Duchess of Malfi. But
in 1827 Lamb only noted (admittedly on one
of Webster's less important plays) what any
antiquary might have done: "Webster was
parish clerk at St Andrew's, Holborn. The
anxious recurrence to church-matters; sacrilege;
tomb-stones; with the frequent introduction of
dirges in this, and his other tragedies, may be
traced to his professional sympathies". The instance is only to be taken partially; but the

desultoriness into which Lamb's new scheme of "Specimens" fell after all is further shown by the fact that he took no trouble to complete all in a volume. The extracts filled up corners of his needy and clever friend Hone's modest magazine *The Table Book*, and there they remained until Lamb's death brought forth a keen demand for his books, which resulted in a new edition of the "Specimens" of 1807 with these last supplements in it.

Since he usually had to be teazed into a new variation on the "Elia" myth,—mystification, or duality, I fail to word this shadow,—it was not likely that he would furnish himself with any new plan requiring continued elaboration for periodical publications; yet he affected once or twice to put on a new purpose. For his friend Stoddart's *New Times* in 1825 he gave himself the title "Lepus", or the hare with many friends, according to the fable; and as Lepus he produced several amusing portraits of human beings, not so dream-fashioned as Elia's usually were, and written with more of the colloquial touch. Here, half in earnest, he protested against the new standardless literary public and the frenzy of the press: "If I hate one day before another, it is the accursed first day of the month, when a load of periodicals is ushered in and distributed to feed the reluctant monster. How it gapes and takes in its prescribed diet, as little savoury as that which Daniel ministered to that Apocryphal dragon, and not more wholesome! Is there no stopping the eternal wheels of the Press for a half century or two, till the nation recover its senses? Must we *magazine* it and *review* it at this sickening rate for ever? Shall we never again read to be *amused*? but to judge, to criticize, to talk about it and about it?" In that there is an intimation of a lost cause, for Lamb had seldom withheld himself from the world of journalism; another taste, or false zeal, had apparently overwhelmed the reserve and discrimination which he and his friends had used. He was glad to see "fair re-prints of good old books"—due in part to his own leading the way; but the fever for new ones as fast as they could be put on the market was the more conspicuous phenomenon.

And still he found a pleasure in being a contributor—and once again he sketched out a small province for his occupation. Through the *New Monthly Magazine* for 1826 he exhibited nineteen "Popular Fallacies", with allusion in the title but not the manner of writing to Sir Thomas Browne's "Vulgar Errors"; he took proverbs for the recreation of juggling with them—and more than that. The series may amount in the main to a small transcript of his fireside talk, and never reappeared as it was first delivered; but there are passages in it which come close to the stature of Lamb's most robust humanity. The paper against the tea-pot platitude "That Home is Home though it is Never so Homely" becomes immediately a description of poverty which uses no epithet of appeal, yet is all appeal; and above all the early lot of the children of the very poor is in his mind's eye. Behind this description we may see one of the causes which took Lamb so frequently on his long walks through the northward suburbs of London, and that anecdote, like the one of Dr Johnson and the printer's boy, of the said Lamb and the grocer's boy. It has nothing mysterious in it; but bears repetition: Lamb sees a small boy struggling towards Islington with a large load of groceries. He removes the load to his own back, and on delivering it asks the lady to intercede with the grocer; she replies, "Sir, I buy my sugar, and have nothing to do with the man's manner of sending it". "Then I hope, ma'am," says the amateur porter, "that you'll give me a drink of small beer"—but the touch was not effective, and the end of the story is Lamb confronting the grocer. Another passage in the "Popular Fallacies" persists—Lamb's retrospect of his experience, which, I hope, corresponds with the reading of his difficult half-century that I have offered here. It occurs in the discussion of Rising with the Lark, which soon becomes only a soliloquy overheard: "Why should we get up? we have neither suit to solicit, nor affairs to manage. The drama has shut in upon us at the fourth act....We were never much in the world. Disappointment early struck a dark veil between us and its dazzling illusions. Our spirits showed grey before our hairs....We have asked no more of life than what the mimic images in play-houses" (one sees Fanny Kelly there bright but sciographic) "present us with. Even those types have waxed fainter. Our clock appears to have struck. We are SUPERANNUATED". That word, once the simple point at which Lamb would have his days to himself, had come to be a harsh curfew, with sullen roar. With the re-signatory confession of which I have repeated a few sentences, there may be associated the day on which John Forster, the biographer-to-be of Dickens, came upon his friend and guide staring up at No. 7, Crown Office Row, Temple. Forster, whose anxious desire to apply tact was not always tact, was forward enough to repeat to Lamb a verse or two he knew,

Ghost-like I paced round the haunts of my childhood,
Earth seemed a desart I was bound to traverse.

No trouble followed; "Yes, boy", said the ghost, smiling on the young and accurate interpreter.

After his *New Monthly* attempt at a new work, Lamb caused some of his friends pain by entering the service of *Blackwood's Magazine*. This powerful Northern monthly had not yet shed all the characteristics of its man-eating youth, but seemed less likely than formerly to destroy a new poet so far as it could, in its antipathy to Reform at large. I fear Lamb did not go into the history of the wars between Maga and the Cockneys when he found that (for example) Blackwood would print "in that same dull Medley...an old rejected farce of mine". This was "The Pawnbroker's Daughter", as good a farce as Saturday night usually provides, but merely extant now as an appendage to its author's other compositions. Why did he publish it? He did not disrelish it, maybe; he may have made a few guineas by it; but it need not be fanciful to see here another instance of his endeavour to maintain a hold on his early intentions. He would have been a writer for the stage, his failure had been unimprovably abrupt—yet still, he was for telling himself that all was not lost. Not for that reason did he come forth soon after—in the year 1830—among the poets once more. The volume was "Album Verses, with a

Few Others", and represents every way the
willingness of Lamb (whenever his "dark companionship" receded from the sunbeam and the
dew) to be the friend of the new generation. So
Wordsworth, and so Coleridge; but Lamb had a
more practical aim, and was shaping one life
above the rest—the publisher Moxon's. Out of
the number of young men of good sense or genius
whom Lamb's paternal instinct sheltered and
blessed through his later days—from Thomas
Hood and Procter and Hartley Coleridge to the
two obscure ones of the India House, Ryle and
Vincent Rice—Moxon was the object of his care.
Lamb had singled him out, in Messrs Longman's
office, by 1826; and now in 1830, with some
money mainly put up by Samuel Rogers, Moxon
was founding his publishing house. He requested Lamb to permit him to bring out, "as a
specimen of the *manner* in which Publications,
entrusted to his care, would appear", a collection
of those rhymes which Lamb, the arch-enemy of
albums and annuals, had written into the albums
of a great many young friends—whose innocent
pleasure vanquished argument. Lamb complied,
and wrote a preface exactly informing the reader
of the situation, and remarking of the poems,
"I feel little interest in their publication. They
are simply—*Advertisement Verses*". This frank-

ness did not save him and his little benevolent
book from an old trick of the reviewers, who
sometimes amuse themselves (and Heaven knows,
reviewers have no excess of amusement) by
avoiding the author's expressed intention and
flogging him for a failure in a race he never ran.
Hence one of the few incidents in public literary
wars with which Lamb's name was latterly associated. In William Jerdan's often ponderous
Literary Gazette—a stubborn weekly journal
which finally yielded to the *Athenaeum*—the
"Album Verses" were made the excuse for an
attack on "the Baa-Lamb School". Southey, who
had last been in the position of Lamb's opponent,
treated this review as an important chance, and
published in *The Times* a poem in Lamb's honour
(with a passing laugh and hardly a polite pun
on the assailant). Hunt equally, in his *Tatler*,
gave Jerdan a volley of epigrams; and the end of
the story is that after a softening reconsideration
of Lamb in a review of Tennyson's poems (which
shows how a decisive new generation now began
to rise above the old), a friendly review of the
"Last Essays of Elia" disclosed that the *Literary
Gazette* was penitent (as suited the public
opinion).

But to return to the "Album Verses"—from
the outside of the book one might say, Is not

this a sorry culmination to the poetical career
which once seemed perhaps promising to rival
those of Coleridge and Wordsworth? From
those romantic Sonnets of the nineteen-year-old
boy, so delicately new and metaphysical, was
there no outcome but "Album Verses"? The
book which Lamb regarded as mere material for
Moxon to print was only in part composed of
rhymes to order, acrostics and ingenuities. The
Advertisement Verses included several which
cannot be refused the title of poems, and at
that such poems as vindicate Lamb from the
charge of utter decline. There were the lines
"In My Own Album" (the metre from Swift
on the Earl of Peterborough), the best of their
kind—for it is not easy to view the subject proposed in a poetical light. Lamb, as some seventeenth-century writer might have conceited it,
instantly saw his Album as an emblem of himself,
and was prepared to illustrate the two together
in clear correspondence, "either other", until
at the close he says his sad goodbye.

> Fresh clad from heaven in robes of white,
> A young probationer of light,
> Thou wert, my soul, an Album bright,
>
> A spotless leaf; but thought, and care,
> And friend and foe, in foul or fair,
> Have "written strange defeatures" there;

And Time, with heaviest hand of all,
Like that fierce writing on the wall,
Hath stamp'd sad dates—he can't recall;

And error, gilding worst designs—
Like speckled snake that strays and shines—
Betrays his path by crooked lines;

And vice hath left his ugly blot;
And good resolves, a moment hot,
Fairly began,—but finish'd not;

And fruitless, late remorse doth trace—
Like Hebrew lore, a backward pace—
Her irrecoverable race.

Disjointed numbers; sense unknit;
Huge reams of folly; shreds of wit;
Compose the mingled mass of it.

My scalded eyes no longer brook
Upon this ink-blurr'd thing to look—
Go, shut the leaves, and clasp the book.

Besides that, which I take to be a good example
of transforming the commonplace into the universal without heavy machinery, Lamb's book
included the profound though direct musing "On
an Infant Dying as Soon as Born" which has
been in many anthologies since, the curious grim
"Gipsy's Malison", and the "Epicedium: Going
or Gone" in which something of Mr Hardy's
faculty to name "local hearts and heads" with

a few words of characterization, and make them
known to us, is seen. The "Epicedium" is incidentally a glimpse of those friendships of Lamb's in
other walks than those of the authors and Londoners which should have been the lifeblood of a
full novel, or a regular autobiography, from him
in these outwardly leisured last years. But apart
from that, and to consider "Album Verses",
what we ask of our poets as much as anything
is simply—individual poems; and here was Lamb
growing old, and far from his former mark, but
able to produce these original poems under the
cover of indifference.

In 1831 through Moxon and anonymously he
published a poem which occupied a volume—
only a brief one—by itself; a poem of which too
little has been said. Its title was "Satan in
Search of a Wife; with the Whole Process of his
Courtship and Marriage, and who Danced at
the Wedding, By an Eye Witness"—and no
doubt its existence was in part due to the "Devil's
Walk" of Coleridge and Southey. Even Leigh
Hunt, not a constitutional opponent of free wit,
reprehended this fantasy as unworthy of the
author of "Elia", and, so doing, exemplified
Lamb's quotation, "you beat but on the case
of Elia"; for the piece has its deeps. *Imprimis*,
it was Lamb's instinctive utterance of indigna-

tion against the spirit of the pre-Victorians,
the tendency to make a boudoir or a Persian
heaven—

> A Persian heaven is easily made,
> It's but black eyes and lemonade—

of the mystery of things.   He resented the
distinctionless Arcadianism of pretty respect-
abilities as a substitute for the substantial
honesty and the strong hopes, faiths and fears
of *his* old home. That was the significance of
his "Dedication": "To delicate bosoms", he
began, "that have sighed over the *Loves of the
Angels*, this Poem is with tenderest regard consecrated. It can be no offence to you, dear Ladies,
that the author has endeavoured to extend the
dominion of your darling passion; to shew Love
triumphant in places, to which his advent has
never yet been suspected....You have fairly
made an Honest Man of the Old One....and we
may sleep for once while at least secure from the
attacks of this hitherto restless Old Bachelor. It
remains to be seen whether the world will be
much benefited by the change in his condition".
That was one aspect of the queer long ballad;
the other, not expressed, but I think no less
certain, was personal to another degree. Occasions
have already arisen for me to suggest the black

conflicts of nervous miscreations which Lamb,
the best humorist of his day, was victim to. The
"thin partitions" specified by Dryden, which in
Mary Lamb so often vanished wildly (stranger
still perhaps that they ever came back!), were
his by nature, and he knew it well; and just as
he had hit on a trick for temporarily beating back
the insanity which menaced Mary—as, in company, he would see her wrong manner and seize
the kettle from the fire and act violence to her
with it suspended over her head—so he devised
his own salvation. Wild talk sometimes—and in
1831 this wild poem—enabled him to exorcize
that other Lamb which he could symbolize as
Sabbathless Satan, to drag that struggling savage
into day, and to treat him with all the tragic
gaiety of his witty puns and comparisons. *Solvi-
tur ambulando*, or rather by dancing over four-
inched bridges; the poem is in the descent of the
seventeenth-century mad songs, with method in
them,—its swaying rhythm mocking, its rhymes
recklessly brilliant, its imagery a medley of great
and little. The mother of Satan is old:

> She remember'd Chaos a little child,
>   Strumming upon hand organs;
> At the birth of Old Night a gossip she sat,
> The ancientest there, and was godmother at
>   The christening of the Gorgons.

Or again, the Devil himself is bedevilled:

> O I perish of cold these bitter sharp nights,
>   The damp like an ague ferrets;
> The ice and the frost hath shot into the bone;
> And I care not greatly to sleep alone
>   O'nights—for the fear of Spirits.

As to the inwardness of the poem, Lamb was moved to tell Moxon that "there was never a year or day in my past life, since I was pen-worthy, that I should not have written precisely as I have"; which surely demands for the understanding of him a perception of *his* Prince of Darkness in it.

Shortly after this revealing caprice Lamb began another protest against the flimsiness of the eighteen-thirties (or rather of the tendency which then became so unescapable) in a prose paper, meant first for part of one of his attempts to unify his energies anew—a series called "Peter's Net". In the breakdown of that wide solution, chance rather than character was prominent; for first of all, Lamb was intending to assist Moxon's excellent *Englishman's Magazine* (which Moxon abruptly gave up), and next, to assist Moxon's *Reflector* (which was abortive and is not known to survive in a single copy). Nevertheless, out of the ruin we have that mighty critical article—a companion-piece

to those of twenty years before on Shakespeare
and on Hogarth—which found out the "Barren-
ness of the Imaginative Faculty in the Productions
of Modern Art" and at the same time gave some
of us our highest approach to the old Masters.
Lamb, of course, in catching up the matter of
criticism of pictures, was in more danger than he
knew. Since his time, it has become almost a
statute that those whose business is writing
can only have a literary, that is a debased and
squinting, attitude towards painting. This new
form of the divine-right theory would probably
not have deterred him much from his impulsive
declaration; and, whatever may be alleged about
the processes of appreciation, there could not be
much doubt of the wisdom of Lamb in the presence of pictures. Already, for instance, he had
said his word about Blake: his word had been the
crowning passage in almost the first general
memoir of Blake (Allan Cunningham's, in the
"British Painters"). "He is the Blake whose
wild designs accompany a splendid edition of
Blair's Grave...; in one of which he pictures the
parting of soul and body by a solid mass of
human form floating off God knows how, from a
lumpish mass—fac-simile to itself—left behind
on the death-bed. He paints in water-colours
marvellous strange pictures—visions of his brain

which he asserts that he has seen. They have
great merit. He has seen the old Welch bards
on Snowdon. He has seen the beautifullest, the
strongest and the ugliest man left alive from
the massacre of the Britons by the Romans, and
has painted them from memory, (I have seen
these paintings), and asserts them to be as good
as the figures of Raphael and Angelo, but not
better....His pictures—one in particular—the
Canterbury Pilgrims, have wonderful power and
spirit, but hard and dry, yet with grace....But
the man is flown, whither I know not—to Hades,
or a mad-house—but I must look on him as one
of the most extraordinary persons of the age."
In view of that extract from a letter, it is strange
that Lamb did not refer to Blake when in 1831
he resolved to dethrone if he might the painter
who then obtained excessive attention as possessed of prodigious imagination—and to challenge prevailing taste through the instance. He
had no special grievance against John Martin,
who was the "amazing" man of that time; and
it is possible to lament the obscurity into which
Martin's gigantical romantical orientalisms and
utopianisms have fallen now, and still to agree
with Lamb, whose business in hand was to point
out what distinguishes the imaginative eye from
the photographic, idea from circumstance. As

before, his doctrine went forth clad in beauties reflected from his themes. I do not know whether he is correct in his interpretation of the "Ariadne" of Titian, but if not he is creatively necessary (for the unassured) to contemplating that picture: "that wonderful bringing together of two times", as he calls it. "Precipitous, with his reeling Satyr rout about him, re-peopling and re-illuming suddenly the waste places, drunk with a new fury beyond the grape, Bacchus, born in fire, fire-like flings himself at the Cretan. This is the time present. With this telling of the story an artist, and no ordinary one, might remain richly proud. Guido, in his harmonious version of it, saw no further. But from the depths of the imaginative spirit Titian has recalled past time, and laid it contributory with the present to one simultaneous effect. With the desert all ringing with the mad cymbals of his followers, made lucid with the presence and new offers of a god,—as if unconscious of Bacchus, or but idly casting her eyes as upon some unconcerning pageant—her soul undistracted from Theseus— Ariadne is still pacing the solitary shore, in as much heart-silence, and in almost the same local solitude, with which she awoke at day-break to catch the forlorn last glances of the sail that bore away the Athenian."

Though Lamb had obliged Moxon to "leave out the sickening Elia" at the end of his "Peter's Net", the essay just mentioned was included in the "Last Essays of Elia", which soon began to be collected for the press. The preparations were spoiled by the anger of John Taylor—become publisher to the London University, his glory lost but his bank balance won —who had published the former "Elia", and now threatened an injunction on the point of copyright. Moxon satisfied Taylor by a payment, and Lamb marked the occasion with one of his finest letters—a malediction in which the ghosts of Luther and of Swift were made to join. For Lamb was not going out of the world without some days equal to any his spirits had expanded to. When his demon was kindly disposed, he was still a youth. Of the "Last Essays" some account has been tried with the others; the book was equal to its predecessor in its supply of classic egoisms, though the Elian figure grew dimmer in its miscellaneous gleanings. It may be a comment in keeping with the subject if I invite you to walk into a bookseller's shop in the summer of 1833, and to see Lamb's last volume among those of the same season—a contrast indeed with the company in which his earliest might have been found. There is not

room to name many such competitors; but these
may be typical: Mrs Austin's "Characteristics of
Goethe", from the German of Falk, 3 volumes:
Captain Medwin's "Shelley Papers"; a new
edition of "Bishop Middleton on the Greek
Article" (one of Lamb's school heroes still
overbrowing him!); Southey's "Naval History
of England", first volume; Captain Thorn-
ton's "History of the East India Company";
"The Encyclopaedia Britannica", 7th edition;
"Encyclopaedia Americana", 13 volumes; "Ar-
cana of Science and Art for 1833"; "The Draw-
ing Room Album" (25 shillings); Nyren's
"Cricketer's Tutor"; Cruikshank's "Sunday in
London"; Lyell's "Principles of Geology",
volume III; Sir J. Herschel's "Treatise on Astro-
nomy"; Gaskell's "Manufacturing Population
of Great Britain, with an examination of Infant
Labour"; Sturt's "Two Expeditions into the
Interior of Southern Australasia"; J. M. W.
Turner's Annual Tour for 1833 (on the Loire);
the Rev. C. Girdlestone's "Seven Sermons on
the Cholera; with a Map"; "The Justice and
Expediency of Substituting an Income and Property Tax for the present Taxes" (anon.); and
let us handle a novel or two (apart from the
torrent of Tales and Romances by the Author of
"Waverley"): "Recollections of a Chaperone,

edited by Lady Dacre" (3 volumes, of course);
"The Parson's Daughter", by—Theodore Hook!
"The New Road to Ruin", by Lady Stepney;
"The Repealers", by Lady Blessington; "Polish
Tales, by the Authoress of Hungarian Tales";
"Golden Legends, containing the Bracelet, the
Locket and the Signet Ring"; and then there
were poetry books, Mrs Lennox Conyngham's
"The Dream and other Poems"; Robert
Montgomery's "Woman the Angel of Life",
and Henry Alford's first book, and the 16th
edition of Tom Moore's least discreet and most
popular lyrics; and the "Rhymed Plea for
Tolerance", by Mrs Browning's friend John
Kenyon; and—not at all likely to displease
Lamb—Dyce's complete edition of the last of
the Elizabethan dramatists, James Shirley. Out
of the vast motley assemblage which the above
list faintly represents, "movement" is ultimately
produced, and literary history organizes its tidy
graphs and paragraphs; and out of it all a few
pages half-grudgingly written down by an isolated man are still very legible.

Here, apart from some oddments given to the
recently established *Athenaeum* (to which also,
if I take the right hint from a letter, Lamb
contributed some money), the story of the
writings which my author published himself

comes to a close. He had never lost his romantic world altogether, but he had not contrived in the period of his retirement to fulfil the double task of imparting that beautiful secret alike to the living who numerously came to his door and to after-comers. It is not necessary to dispense blame and praise between him and his contemporaries on this ultimate elusiveness compared with what they did, or were. The instance has yet to be produced of a man who, directing his personal life with such discipline as Lamb, volunteering so valiantly and maintaining what he had volunteered for, sharing himself so tirelessly every way yet always with particularity of regard, even shaping himself with resolute and grumbling pertinacity into a skilful practitioner in a task he was not made for, yet guarded an original spirit in literature into his age, and made his latest fragments prove, "there is not any severing of our loves". It is scarcely necessary to dwell on the homelessness of his last years, still lived for his sister,[1] whose lucid

[1] A statement of Mrs Moxon's, who as Emma Isola lived so long with the Lambs, expresses well the difficulty and the courage of their life. While she was with them, she was completely ignorant of the tragedy of their mother. "One night, Charles and Mary Lamb were seated at table. The conversation

intervals grew briefer. "In short," he cried to Wordsworth in 1834, "I may call her half dead to me." What ended him was, as some observed, the departure of Coleridge on July 25th, 1834. They had begun their thinking and writing life together. On November 21st, when Lamb was desired to write a page in an album, he could only remember the subject that had interrupted all his talk for months: he composed the brief and reverent prose elegy which everybody knows as well as his former jests on Coleridge's pecca-dillos. And Coleridge had been moved, one day before his last illness, to speak of Lamb more nearly than he had been heard to do; that utter-ance is not, I believe, over-familiar: "Charles Lamb has more totality and individuality of character than any other man I know, or have ever known in all my life. In most men we dis-tinguish between the different powers of their intellect as one being predominant over the other. The genius of Wordsworth is greater than his talent, though considerable. The talent of Southey is greater than his genius, though respectable;

turned on the elder Lamb, when Miss Isola asked why she never heard mention of the mother. Mary thereupon uttered a sharp, piercing cry, for which Charles playfully and laughingly rebuked her; but he made no allusion to the cause."

and so on. But in Charles Lamb it is altogether
one; his genius is talent, and his talent is genius,
and his heart is as whole and as one as his head.
The wild words that come from him sometimes
on religious subjects would shock you from the
mouth of any other man, but from him they seem
mere flashes of firework. If an argument seem
to his reason not fully true, he bursts out in that
odd desecrating way; yet his will, the inward
man, is, I well know, profoundly religious.
Watch him when alone, and you will find him
with either a Bible, or an old divine, or an old
English poet; in such is his pleasure".

After Lamb's death[1] (on December 27th, 1834)

[1] A glimpse of him in his last days may find a
place in a note, though, like all else in the recollections
of him then, it does not discern the real nature of his
restlessness.

"Lamb passed the last period of his life in the
village, or more soundingly, the 'Hundred' of Edmonton. To a native of that same rusticity, and an
occasional resident, it was a strange yet consistent
sight to observe the form in 'clerk-like black' taking
a regular morning walk on the dusty London road,
instead of diving into the shady sweetness of the
green lanes. But we saw his wistful, half-averted
glances at the coaches that passed city-ward, and felt
his yearnings towards the scenes of his youth. He
died in consequence of a trifling accident that

there was great rivalry among his friends which
should write best of him; Barron Field, Forster,
Procter, Moxon, Leigh Hunt, Talfourd (more
extensively and officially), Cary (in verse),
Wordsworth and George Dyer ("Amicus Re-

happened to him during one of these walks, and
was buried in Edmonton churchyard. He had pointed
out the spot himself a short time before while walking
there with his sister, 'as the place where he wished to
be buried'. The spot is by no means romantic, though
something of the kind might easily have been found
among the mossy, mouldering, carved vaults and
tombs at remote corners, beneath old yew trees,
dense blackthorn hedges, or beside the venerable
buttresses of the old church walls. Lamb, however,
preferred to be located, not only where the place
was pretty thick with companionable tombs, but
where he could be nearer the walks of human life.
His grave-stone accordingly stands, at a little dis-
tance, facing a footpath which leads to the lanes and
fields at the back of the church. The inscription upon
it is simply 'To the memory of Charles Lamb. Died
27 Dec. 1834: aged 59'. There, in fixed peaceful-
ness, among a crowd of familiar names—names
known from infancy—we often see it stand with
pallid smile just after sunset, while sparrows fly
chirrupping from tomb to tomb, and ruminating sheep
recline with half-closed eyes against the warm, flat
stone, or grassy mound."

British and Foreign Review.

divivus" (he characteristically wrote his tribute twice) at once occur to my mind. And Lamb, the humanist, became a popular author,—was even published at Paris in 1835. The Victorian age was coming in, not the most propitious, one might have said, thinking of the broadness of Dickens, the stoniness of Carlyle, the *quod erat demonstrandum* of Macaulay and the high calling of Ruskin, for the growth of this man's fame through the enjoyment of his fine lights and shades. It was worth Macaulay's while, nevertheless, to turn his guns on one of Elia's dexterous fabrics; Pickwick did not superannuate Elia; Carlyle on Lamb's humour was felt to be a little solemn; and only now, when possibly we may perceive a change in human preoccupations, and when from many causes a literature of the smash-and-grab type or the semi-scientific seems to have some chance of superseding the thorough, persuasive, modulated and interwoven style, may a note of foreboding just sound in one more of the descants on Charles Lamb the very reasonable romantic.

INDEX

www.ingramcontent.com/pod-product-compliance
Ingram Content Group UK Ltd.
Pitfield, Milton Keynes, MK11 3LW, UK
UKHW042143280225
455719UK00001B/54